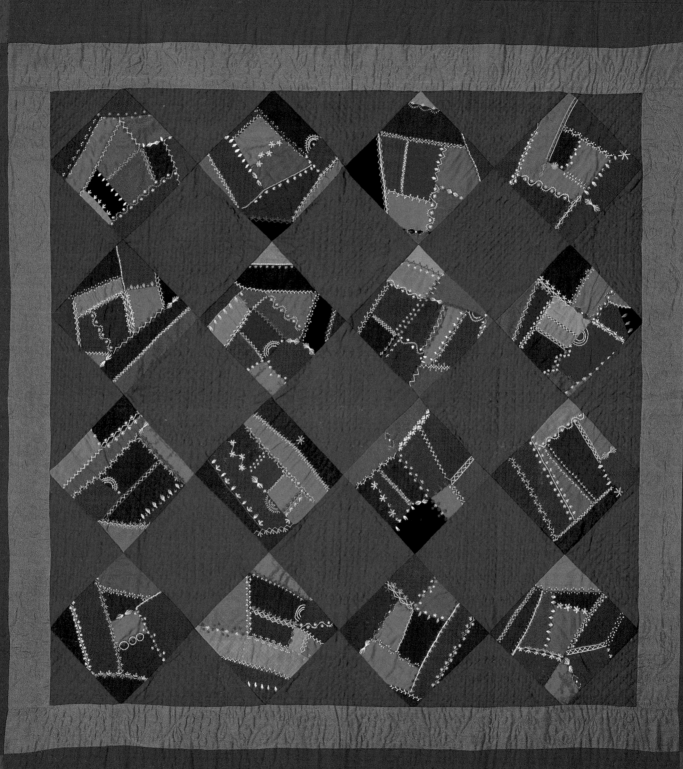

"Reflections of our Heritage"
AFRO-AMERICAN QUILTERS OF LOS ANGELES
POST OFFICE BOX 781213
LOS ANGELES, CA 90016-9213

AAQLA
AFRO AMERICAN QUILTERS OF
L A

A Quiet Spirit

AMISH QUILTS
FROM THE COLLECTION OF
CINDY TIETZE & STUART HODOSH

Donald B. Kraybill

Patricia T. Herr

Jonathan Holstein

UCLA FOWLER MUSEUM OF CULTURAL HISTORY

THIS PUBLICATION AND ASSOCIATED EXHIBITION WERE SUPPORTED BY FUNDING FROM

Bradley A. Jabour, Medical Imaging Center of Southern California
Intermedics, Inc., A Company of SULZER*medica*
Barry A. Kitnick and Jill Alexander Kitnick
The Times-Mirror Foundation
The Ahmanson Foundation
Manus, the Support Group of the UCLA Fowler Museum of Cultural History

DANIEL R. BRAUER *Design*
CORINNE LIGHTWEAVER *Editing*
DENIS J. NERVIG *Photography*
JENNIFER M. LEES *Project Assistant*

© 1996 REGENTS OF THE UNIVERSITY OF CALIFORNIA

UCLA FOWLER MUSEUM OF CULTURAL HISTORY
BOX 951549
LOS ANGELES, CALIFORNIA, USA 90095-1549

PRINTED AND BOUND IN HONG KONG
BY SOUTH SEA INTERNATIONAL PRESS, LTD.

Library of Congress Cataloging-in-Publication Data

Kraybill, Donald B.
     A quiet spirit: Amish quilts from the collection of Cindy Tietze and Stuart
Hodosh / Donald B. Kraybill, Patricia T. Herr, Jonathan Holstein.
          p. cm.
     Exhibition catalog.
     Includes bibliographical references.
     ISBN 0-930741-52-8 (hard). — ISBN 0-930741-53-6 (soft).
     1. Quilts, Amish—Exhibitions. 2. Tietze, Cindy—Art collections—
Exhibitions. 3. Hodosh, Stuart—Art collections—Exhibitions. 4. Quilts—
Private collections—New York (State)—New York—Exhibitions.
1. Herr, Patricia T., 1936- . II. Holstein, Jonathan. III. Title.
NK9112.K73 1996   96-30790
746.46'074794'94—dc20   CIP

DEDICATION

Mary Beth and Albert Tietze
Frances and David Hodosh

HONOR THY FATHER AND MOTHER

Cindy Tietze
Stuart Hodosh

Contents

9   Acknowledgments

13   The Quiltwork of Amish Culture
DONALD B. KRAYBILL

45   Quilts within the Amish Culture
PATRICIA T. HERR

69   In Plain Sight: The Aesthetics of Amish Quilts
JONATHAN HOLSTEIN

123   Catalog
AMISH QUILTS FROM THE COLLECTION
OF CINDY TIETZE & STUART HODOSH

228   References Cited

Acknowledgments

With my first view of the Amish quilts from the collection of Cindy Tietze and Stuart Hodosh, I was absolutely captivated. Each work seemed more breathtaking than the one before. Museums rarely have the opportunity to exhibit material put together with such intelligence and taste. I would like to thank Cindy and Stuart for sharing their collection with our audience and for being such engaging and enthusiastic colleagues in the process. It was a joy working with them; their efforts and generosity are sincerely appreciated.

Donald B. Kraybill, Patricia T. Herr, and Jonathan Holstein brought their unique expertise and thoughtful prose to the publication to provide history and context for the quilts. Their affection for the subject is clearly apparent and we are grateful for their insights and diligence. It has been an honor to work with such professionals. Corinne Lightweaver edited this volume with characteristic skill and sensitivity.

The remarkable photographs of Susan Einstein that grace the pages of Donald Kraybill's essay were the subject of a companion exhibition, "Views of an Amish Community." Susan was staff photographer at the Museum in the 1970s and it was a pleasure working with her again. Her observations and reflections on Amish life in Indiana are greatly valued contributions.

David Mayo created both exhibitions with typical perceptiveness and flair. His installations continue to engage both the mind and the eye. The educational agendas were developed by Betsy Quick, whose interpretive approach communicated vitality and insight to our richly diverse audiences. Both David and Betsy shared curatorial responsibilities with me and, as always, they are the best of collaborators.

This catalog was beautifully designed by Danny Brauer whose sense of invention and surprise has sustained the Museum's publication program for the last eight years. Photographing quilts is a special challenge. Denis Nervig has carefully captured the relief and detail of the dramatic works of art seen on these pages. As always, the rest of the Museum staff performed to perfection. Their combined efforts continue to amaze.

Funding for the exhibition was generously provided by Bradley A. Jabour of the Medical Imaging Center of Southern California; Intermedics, Inc., A Company of SULZER*medica*; and Jill and Barry Kitnick. Additional support came from Museum Endowment Funds generated by the

Ahmanson Foundation and The Times-Mirror Foundation. This project would not have been possible without all of their participation.

The art of quilting has engaged the staff of the UCLA Fowler Museum of Cultural History since its founding in 1963 under the name of the Museum and Laboratories of Ethnic Arts and Technology and under the leadership of the late Ralph Altman. The textile collections of the Museum were built in large part through the initiatives of Curator Emeritus Patricia Altman. She was also responsible for starting a tradition within the Museum that produced quilts to commemorate births and weddings, with each staff member creating a square for the quilt. The tenth anniversary of the Museum was distinguished with a collaborative quilt featuring a work from the collection on each square in the style of a Victorian crazy quilt.

When the opportunity arose to exhibit the Amish quilts from the collection of Cindy Tietze and Stuart Hodosh, Pat Altman enthusiastically endorsed the project as she has so many other textile initiatives within the Museum. I would like to thank Pat for her many efforts over the years to enlarge the Museum's textile holdings, creating one of the finest collections in the world, and for curating many stunning exhibitions. Her tenure at the Museum has exceeded that of any other staff member and she has continued to be our greatest supporter.

Doran H. Ross
DIRECTOR

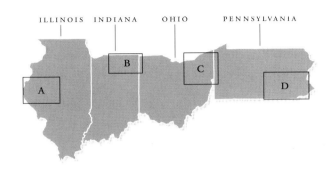

ILLINOIS INDIANA OHIO PENNSYLVANIA

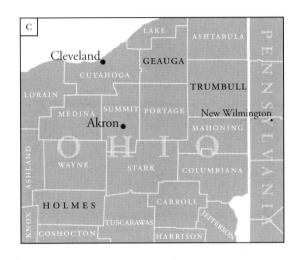

C

LAKE ASHTABULA

Cleveland
CUYAHOGA GEAUGA

PENNSYLVANIA

LORAIN

MEDINA SUMMIT PORTAGE TRUMBULL

New Wilmington

Akron
MAHONING

ASHLAND

WAYNE STARK COLUMBIANA

O H I O

KNOX HOLMES CARROLL JEFFERSON

COSHOCTON TUSCARAWAS HARRISON

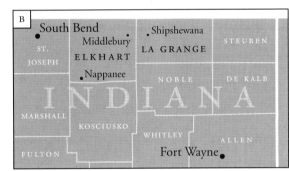

B

South Bend
ST.
JOSEPH

Middlebury
ELKHART LA GRANGE

Shipshewana

STEUBEN

Nappanee

NOBLE DE KALB

MARSHALL

I N D I A N A

KOSCIUSKO

WHITLEY ALLEN

FULTON Fort Wayne

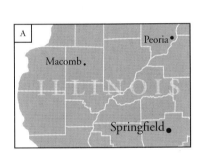

A

Peoria

Macomb

I L L I N O I S

Springfield

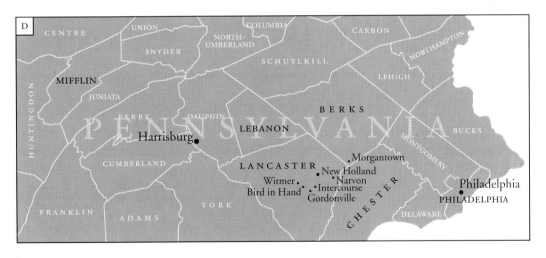

D

CENTRE UNION COLUMBIA CARBON

SNYDER NORTH-
UMBERLAND SCHUYLKILL NORTHAMPTON

MIFFLIN LEHIGH

HUNTINGDON JUNIATA

PERRY DAUPHIN BERKS BUCKS

P E N N S Y L V A N I A

LEBANON MONTGOMERY

Harrisburg

CUMBERLAND Morgantown

LANCASTER New Holland

Philadelphia

Witmer Narvon

Bird in Hand Intercourse CHESTER PHILADELPHIA

FRANKLIN YORK Gordonville

ADAMS DELAWARE

11

The Quiltwork
of Amish Culture

Donald B. Kraybill

EUROPEAN BEGINNINGS

The Amish stem from Swiss Anabaptists who emerged during the Protestant Reformation in sixteenth-century Europe. Dubbed Anabaptists or "twice baptizers" by their opponents, these radical reformers called for a sharp separation of church and state. They insisted on adult or rebaptism despite being baptized as infants by the Catholic Church. Unhappy with the sluggish pace of the larger Reformation, the Anabaptists declared that the authority of the scriptures superseded the mandates of civil government. Taking a literal view of New Testament teachings, the Anabaptists called for obedient discipleship—daily devotion—to the ways of Jesus.[1]

The youthful reformers challenged, indeed threatened, the hegemony of church and state by rejecting infant baptism, refusing to take oaths of allegiance, and renouncing military conscription. This so-called radical wing of the Reformation criticized the lax ethical life of trained clergy and rejected many of the accepted rituals and practices of both Catholic and emerging Protestant churches. Declaring many of the time-honored rituals "idolatrous," the Anabaptists emphasized the practice of Christian faith in daily life. The Anabaptist movement started in 1525 in Zurich, Switzerland but soon appeared in southern Germany, Moravia, the Netherlands, and in other regions of Western Europe.

The Anabaptist challenge to the age-old marriage of church and state did not go unheeded. Civil and religious authorities responded with a vicious campaign to eradicate the "pernicious sect." Anabaptist hunters stalked the land looking for the heretics who dared to challenge the very bedrock of civil authority. Between 1525 and 1600, thousands of Anabaptists lost their heads to the executioner's sword, died in prison, burned at the stake, drowned in rivers, and endured innumerable forms of torture for their religious faith.

The story of this bloody theater is recorded in the 1,200-page *Martyrs Mirror*, first published in Dutch in 1660 and later in German and English (FIG. 1). Copies of *Martyrs Mirror*, often found

OPPOSITE: Detail of CAT. 18

in Amish homes, keep the memories of persecution fresh among the Amish today. The severe persecution in Europe galvanized a sharp separation between Anabaptist ways and the culture of the larger world. Thus the theme of separation from the world, legitimated by numerous biblical passages, became a bulwark in Amish culture and undergirds much of their life today.

The most prominent religious groups that trace their roots to the Anabaptist movement of sixteenth-century Europe include the Hutterites, Mennonites, and Amish. The Hutterites, named for Anabaptist leader Jacob Hutter, rejected private property and formed their own communities in the second quarter of the sixteenth century. Today they live in some 400 agricultural communes in North America, primarily in the Dakotas and in several Canadian provinces.

Various Mennonite groups, scattered around the globe, also trace their lineage to the Radical Reformation. They take their name from Menno Simons, a Dutch priest, who converted to Anabaptism in 1536 and became an influential preacher and writer. Some Old Order Mennonites share similar practices with the Amish, but over the years many Mennonites have drifted into the cultural mainstream. Mainstream Mennonites use state-of-the-art technology, endorse higher education, pursue professional occupations, and, apart from pacifism, have assimilated into many aspects of modern life.

The Amish emerged as a distinctive group in 1693, following a rift within the Anabaptist family that led to Amish and Mennonite factions. The Amish were named for Jakob Ammann, a Swiss-born elder, who played a central role in the schism that tore the Swiss and South German Anabaptists asunder in the 1690s.[2] Amish congregations formed in Switzerland and northward along the Rhine River in the Alsace and Palatinate areas of present-day France and Germany.

1. In *Martyrs Mirror*, Amish read the story of Anneken Hendriks, a housewife from Frisia who was betrayed by an Anabaptist Judas and put to death by fire in 1571 in Amsterdam. Hendriks was one of thousands of Anabaptists who were tortured and executed for their so-called heretical religious beliefs.

Original etching by Mennonite artist Jan Luyken for the 1685 edition of *Martyrs Mirror*

The religious fervor of early Anabaptism gradually waned between 1525 and 1690 under harsh persecution and the realities of everyday living. Ammann and other leaders proposed several reforms to revitalize church life by strengthening congregational discipline, which in their view had grown lax. An acrimonious division was triggered by doctrinal disputes, personality conflicts, procedural snafus, regional differences, and a variety of sociocultural factors.

Jakob Ammann and others hoped to reform the church in several ways. To promote doctrinal purity and spiritual rigor they proposed stricter measures of congregational discipline and emphasized a sharp separation between church and world. Appealing to New Testament teachings and the practice of Dutch Anabaptists, Ammann advocated shunning excommunicated members in table fellowship and in daily life. The Swiss Anabaptists typically excluded wayward members from communion but did not avoid them in social affairs. Following the Dutch Anabaptists, Ammann also argued that Christians, in obedience to the teachings of Christ, should wash each others' feet in the communion service.

Despite several differences, the contention over shunning drove the decisive wedge between

Ammann's followers and the established Swiss leaders. The social and theological differences as well as personal entanglements produced a permanent breech among the Swiss-South German Anabaptists. Ammann's followers were eventually called Amish while descendants of other Swiss-German Anabaptists eventually took the name Mennonite. Although sharing a common lineage, the Amish and Mennonites have held separate identities since 1693. Although the Amish carried the banner of reform at their origin, their accents on congregational discipline and church-world separation have fostered a traditional and conservative culture over the centuries.

GROWTH IN NORTH AMERICA

Searching for political stability and religious freedom, the Amish came to North America in the mid-eighteenth century and again in a second wave of migration in the first half of the nineteenth century. Their first settlements took root in southeastern Pennsylvania, but in time they followed the frontier to other counties in Pennsylvania and then on to Ohio, Indiana, and other Midwestern states. In Europe, the last Amish congregation dissolved in 1937. Amish settlements today cluster in the mid-Atlantic and Midwestern regions of the country.

The "Old Order" label emerged in the latter half of the nineteenth century in the throes of an Amish schism in North America. Clusters of progressively inclined Amish in some communities formed new congregations which eventually merged with mainstream Mennonite churches.[3] The conservers who upheld traditional Amish ways became known as the Old Order Amish. About a century later, in the 1960s and 1970s, some so-called New Order Amish left the Old Order fold to establish their own congregations in Ohio. In the following years New Order congregations formed in other states as well.

The New Order Amish represent less than ten percent of the total Amish family today. New Order groups accept more modern conveniences, encourage personal Bible study, and advocate stricter moral standards for their youth. The New Orders typically permit their members to install phones in their homes, tap electricity from public utilities, and use tractors in the field. They have Sunday schools and organized activities for their youth. The largest concentration of New Order Amish resides in the Holmes County area of Ohio.

The Old Order Amish have enjoyed remarkable growth in twentieth-century North America. Despite their tenacity for traditional ways they have thrived amid the most technologically advanced century of all time. At the turn of the century they numbered some 5,000, but today nearly 150,000 children and adults and are scattered across 22 states and into Ontario. Nearly three-quarters live in Ohio, Pennsylvania, and Indiana, with other sizable communities in Iowa, Michigan, Missouri, New York, and Wisconsin.[4]

In recent years their population has doubled about every 20 years. The decade of 1981 to 1991 witnessed an increase of 329 congregations, about 33 new ones per year.[5] Amish historian David Luthy reports that the Amish established about 145 new settlements in the 20-year period between 1972 and 1992.[6] By the early 1990s migration initiatives had scattered them into 220 geographical settlements in the United States and seven in Ontario.

A loose federation of nearly 1,000 congregations functions without a national organization or an annual convention. Local church districts—congregations of 25 to 35 families—shape the heart

2. The Amish have historically been a people of the land. Until recently, agriculture was their main means of living.

Photograph by Susan Einstein,
Elkhart-LaGrange Counties, Indiana, 1981-1984

of Amish life. Congregations with similar practices permit their ministers to preach in each others' services and are considered "in fellowship" with each other. These loose networks of like-minded congregations are typically called affiliations. Specific practices vary considerably from region to region and between the different affiliations.

DISTINCTIVE AND DIVERSE

All Amish groups speak a German dialect, originating in the Palatinate area along the Rhine River. The dialect, known as Pennsylvania German, is sometimes nicknamed Pennsylvania Dutch (Deutsch). Children learn English and German in school, but the dialect is the currency of work, play, and worship. Outsiders are typically referred to as "English," reflecting the importance of the language boundary. The Amish have created a distinctive identity by maintaining sharp boundaries around their community. The symbols of separation carve deep contours between their sectarian subculture and the larger society, bestowing a firm sense of meaning, belonging, and identity that bolsters their collective loyalty.

At least ten badges of identity are shared by most Old Order Amish groups across North America. These symbols of separation which project a uniform public front include the following: horse and buggy transportation, the use of horses and mules for field work, plain dress in many variations, a beard but no mustache for men, a prayer cap for women, the Pennsylvania German dialect, worship in homes, parochial schooling through the eighth grade, the rejection of electricity from public utility lines, and taboos on the ownership of televisions and computers. These symbols of solidarity circumscribe the Amish world, mark it off from the larger society, and help to

3. The horse and buggy, one of the most distinguishing badges of Amish identity, reflect the desire to remain separate from the modern world and the rejection of some forms of technology.

Photograph by Susan Einstein, Elkhart-LaGrange Counties, Indiana, 1981-1984

bridle the forces of cultural assimilation.

Amish life is regulated by the *Ordnung*, an unwritten code of conduct. An informal cluster of understandings, the Ordnung embodies the taboos and behavioral expectations which shape Amish life. It covers aspects of Amish life ranging from attire to the use of technology including pre-scriptions related to dress—a prayer covering for women and a regulation hat for men, as well as proscriptions: the Amish may not own a television, hold a driver's license, or attend high school. The particulars of the Ordnung vary from community to community. For example, in some settle-ments the buggy tops are black, but in others they are yellow. Children learn the ways of the Ordnung at an early age by observation and imitation. Church leaders occasionally revise the guide-lines of the Ordnung as they struggle with new issues and face new forms of technology.

The Amish church prescribes dress regulations for its members but the standards vary from settlement to settlement. Men are expected to wear a wide brim hat and a vest when they appear in public. In winter months and at church services they wear a black suit coat, typically fastened with hooks and eyes rather than with buttons. The men also use suspenders instead of belts. Modern styled, commercially tailored suits and ties are forbidden.

Amish women are expected to wear a prayer covering and a bonnet when they appear in pub-lic settings. Most women wear a cape over the top of their dress as well as an apron. The three parts of the dress are typically fastened together with straight pins. Various colors—green, brown, blue, lavender—are permitted for women's dresses and men's shirts but designs and figures on fabrics are taboo. Although very young girls do not wear a prayer covering, Amish children typically dress similarly to their parents. All forms of facial makeup and jewelry, including wedding rings and

5. Horses working in the field.

Photograph by Susan Einstein,
Elkhart-LaGrange Counties, Indiana, 1981-1984

wristwatches are forbidden. The unique patterns of costume worn by the Amish give them a distinctive public identity.

At first glance all Amish groups appear identical—pressed from the same cultural mold. A deeper look, however, reveals many differences among them. Some affiliations forbid milking machines while others depend on them. Mechanical hay balers, pulled by horses across some Amish fields, are taboo in others. Mules are used for field work in some areas but forbidden in others. Prescribed buggy tops are gray or black in many affiliations but white or yellow in others. Buttons on clothing, banished in many groups, are accepted in the more progressive ones. Gas refrigerators are welcomed by some groups but forbidden by others. One group insists that men wear one suspender. The dead are embalmed in some settlements but not in others.

Practices vary between congregations, even within the same settlement. Some bishops permit telephones in small shops, but others do not. Artificial insemination of livestock is acceptable in one district but not in another. In some communities most of the men are farmers but in other regions the majority work in small shops and cottage industries. In the Elkhart-LaGrange settlement of Indiana many Amish persons work in rural factories operated by non-Amish persons. Endless diversity, with dozens of distinctions within and between subgroups, thrives behind the common badges of identity that appear on the front stage of Amish life.

4 (OPPOSITE). Elder Amish man.

Photograph by Susan Einstein,
Elkhart-LaGrange Counties, Indiana, 1981-1984

THE QUILTWORK OF AMISH VALUES

Lovely Amish quilts symbolize the patchwork of Amish culture—the memories, myths, and beliefs that shape the Amish world. The value structure of Amish life pivots on *Gelassenheit* (pronounced ge-las-en-hite)—the cornerstone of Amish values. Roughly translated, the German word means submission—yielding to a higher authority. Gelassenheit entails self-surrender, resignation to God's will, yielding to others, self-denial, contentment, and a quiet spirit. For early Anabaptists, Gelassenheit meant forsaking all ambition and yielding fully to God's will—even unto death. Christ called them to abandon self-interests and follow his example of humility, service, and suffering. The religious meaning of Gelassenheit expresses itself in a quiet and reserved personality and places the needs of others above self. Gelassenheit nurtures a subdued self with gentle handshakes, lower voices, slower strides—a life etched with modesty and reserve.

This way of thinking—yielding to God and others—permeates Amish culture. It undergirds values, personality, symbols, rituals, and social patterns. Children learn the essence of Gelassenheit in a favorite schoolroom verse:

> I must be a Christian child,
> Gentle, patient, meek, and mild,
> Must be honest, simple, true,
> I must cheerfully obey,
> Giving up my will and way…

Another favorite saying notes that "JOY" means Jesus first, Yourself last, and Others in between. Eager to discourage individualism and pride, Amish teachers remind students that the middle letter of pride is I. As the cornerstone of Amish culture, Gelassenheit collides with the bold, assertive individualism of modern life that seeks and rewards personal achievement, self-fulfillment, and individual recognition at every turn.

The spirit of Gelassenheit expresses itself in obedience, humility, and simplicity. To Amish thinking, obedience to the will of God is the cardinal religious value. Disobedience is dangerous. Unconfessed it leads to eternal separation. Submission to authority at all levels creates an orderly community. Children learn to obey at an early age as disobedience is "nipped in the bud." Students obey teachers without question, adults yield to the regulations of the church, and ministers concede to bishops. Obedience to divine and human authority regulates social relationships from the youngest child to the oldest bishop, who in turn obeys the Lord.

Humility is coupled with obedience in Amish life. Pride, a religious term for unbridled individualism, threatens the welfare of an orderly community. Proud individuals display the spirit of arrogance, not Gelassenheit. They "show off," trying to get attention and taking all the credit. They are pushy, bold, forward, and always "jumping the fence." What moderns consider proper credit for personal accomplishment the Amish view as the hankerings of a vain spirit. Proud individuals tack their name on everything, promote personal accomplishments, draw attention to themselves, seek recognition in the press, hang personal portraits, and take credit for everything. The sinister head of pride disturbs the equality and tranquility of an orderly community while the humble person freely gives of self in the service of community without seeking recognition.

Simplicity is also esteemed in Amish life. Fancy and gaudy decorations lead to pride. Simplicity in clothing, household decor, architecture, and worship nurtures equality and orderliness. Sacrifice signals a yielded self; luxury and convenience cultivate vanity. The fluff of pretentious display

reflects the haughty spirit of the outside world. The tools of self-adornment—make-up, jewelry, wristwatches, and wedding rings—are taboo. These cosmetic props, signs of pride, encourage pushy selves to show off "number one." Modern dress accents individual expression and social status. By contrast, Amish dress signals submission to the collective order. Common garb symbolizes a yielded self and promotes order and equality.

Bending to the call of community, however, does not smother individual expression. Outside observers are often surprised by the amount of individual freedom within the boundaries of Amish society. The Amish neither wallow in self-contempt nor champion wilted personalities. What they lose in the freedom of self-expression they gain in a durable ethnic identity embedded in a caring community.

The values in the quiltwork of Amish culture are stitched together by separation from the world. Galvanized by European persecution and sanctioned by scripture, the Amish divide the social world into two pathways: the straight and narrow way to life, and the broad and easy road to destruction. Amish life embodies the narrow way of self-denial. The larger social world represents the broad road of vanity and vice. The term world, in Amish thinking, refers to the outside society—its values, vices, practices, and institutions. Media reports of greed, fraud, scandal, drugs, violence, divorce, and abuse confirm, in Amish minds, a world teeming with abomination.

The gulf between church and world, imprinted in Amish minds by decades of persecution, guides practical decisions. The separatist impulse infuses Amish thinking and steers decision-making. Products and practices which might undermine community life—high school, cars, cameras, television, and self-propelled farm machinery—are tagged worldly. Many new products do not receive the pejorative label, only those that threaten community values. Definitions of worldliness vary within and between Amish settlements, yielding a complicated morass of practices. Baffling to the outsider, these lines of faithfulness maintain intergroup boundaries and also preserve the purity of the church. Despite their collective commitment to remain separate from the world, many Amish persons develop congenial friendships with neighbors and outsiders on a personal level.

Amish society pivots on a delicate tension between tradition and social change. In a consumer world where new is considered better, the Amish tilt toward the past. Said one minister, "We consider tradition as being spiritually helpful.... There is a lot of value in tradition and we realize that." In the words of another, "Tradition to us is a sacred trust. It is part of our religion to uphold and adhere to the ideals of our forefathers." Modern societies face forward and plan their futures, whereas the Amish treasure tradition as a resource for coping with the present. "Tradition," noted an Amish man, "puts a brake on the dangerous wheel of social change."

The quiltwork of Amish values—obedience, humility, simplicity, separation from the world, and esteem for tradition—undergirds their vision for an orderly and contented community. These are ideal values. Like all human communities, gaps appear between the ideal and the real. Greed lifts its head at times. Jealousy and envy sometimes flare. Rowdy youth occasionally irritate and embarrass community elders. Marriages can sour, and interpersonal feuds sometimes tear a congregation asunder. Splits and divisions, often spurred by efforts to preserve the purity of the church, sometimes bring conflict. Beneath the peaceful quiltwork of Amish ideals, these people are people.

PATTERNS OF SOCIAL ORGANIZATION

The immediate family, extended family, and church district form the basic building blocks of Amish society. Amish parents typically raise about seven children, although ten or more is not uncommon. About 50 percent of the population is under 18 years of age. An Amish person often has 75 or more first cousins, and a typical grandmother easily counts more than 35 grandchildren. Members of the extended family often live nearby. Youth grow up in this thicket of family relations where, as one Amish woman put it, "everyone knows everyone else's business." One is rarely alone, but always embedded in a caring community in time of need and disaster. The elderly retire at home, usually in a small apartment attached to the main house of a homestead. Thus from cradle to grave the community provides a supportive social hammock.

Twenty-five to 35 families living in proximity constitute a church district or congregation, the basic social and religious unit beyond the family. Roads and streams mark the boundaries of church districts. Members participate in the district surrounding their home. A district's geographic size varies with the density of the Amish population. In smaller districts families often walk to church services which rotate among the homes of members. As districts grow, they divide. A bishop, two preachers, and a deacon, without formal education or salary, share leadership responsibilities in each congregation. The bishop, as spiritual elder, officiates at baptisms, weddings, communions, funerals, ordinations, and membership meetings. The local district—the hub of Amish life—is neighborhood, club, family, and precinct all wrapped up into a neighborhood parish. Periodic meetings of ordained leaders link the districts of a settlement into a loose federation.

Amish society is patriarchal. Apart from schoolteachers, who are generally women, men assume the helm of most leadership roles. Although they can nominate men to serve in ministerial roles, women are excluded from formal church roles. Women can, however, vote in church business meetings. Some women feel that, since "the men make the rules," modern technology is sometimes permitted more readily in barns and shops than in homes. In recent years some women have taken on new roles as entrepreneurs, establishing quilting operations, craft stores, roadside stands, and food stores.[7]

Although husband and wife preside over distinct spheres of domestic life, many tasks are shared. A wife may ask her husband to assist in the garden and he may ask her to help in the barn, field, or shop. The isolated housewife, trapped in the kitchen of industrial societies, is rarely found in Amish society. The husband does hold spiritual authority in the home but spouses have considerable freedom within their distinctive spheres. In the words of one Amish man, "The wife is not a servant; she is the queen and the husband is the king." The extent of mutuality between husband and wife, as in other societies, varies considerably with personalities.

Social life—leisure, work, education, play, worship, and friendship—revolves around the immediate neighborhood. Amish babies in some settlements are born in hospitals, but many of them greet this world at home or in local birthing centers. Weddings and funerals occur at home. There are frequent trips to other settlements or even out of state to visit relatives and friends. But for the most part, the Amish world pivots on local turf. From home-canned food to homemade haircuts, things are likely to be done at or near home. Social relationships are multibonded; the same people frequently work, play, and worship together. Unlike the fragmented networks of modern life, the Amish are tied into overlapping circles of friendship.

Amish society is remarkably informal. Without a centralized national office, a symbolic national leader, or an annual convention, the tentacles of bureaucracy are sparse. Apart from one-room schools, a modest publishing operation, and a few historical libraries, formal institutions do not exist. A loosely organized national steering committee provides a common voice for dealing with various government agencies.[8] Regional committees in various areas coordinate activities related to schools, mutual aid, and historical interests, but typical bureaucratic structures are nonexistent in Amish life.

From egos to organizational units, Amish society reflects the small-scale spirit of humility. The Amish limit the size of congregations to about 35 households by meeting in their homes for worship. Farms, shops, and schools are also relatively small. Small-scale social units increase informality and participation and prevent power from accumulating on the lap of one person. Moreover, small-scale settings provide each person an emotional niche within a network of social support.

The conventional marks of social status—education, income, occupation, and consumer goods—are largely missing from Amish society. Their agrarian heritage placed most members on common social footing. Today, however, the rise of small industries in some settlements and factory work in others threatens the social equality of bygone years. Nevertheless, the range of occupations and social differences remains relatively small. Common costume, horse and buggy travel, an eighth-grade education, and equal-size tombstones symbolize the virtues of equality despite growing economic disparity produced by off-farm employment.

The practice of mutual aid also distinguishes Amish society. Although the Amish own private property, they have long emphasized mutual aid as a Christian duty in the face of disaster and special need. Mutual aid goes far beyond romanticized barn raisings; harvesting, quilting, births, weddings, and funerals require the help of many hands. The habits of care encompass all sorts of needs triggered by drought, disease, death, injury, and bankruptcy, as well as medical emergency. The community springs into spontaneous action in these moments of despair—articulating the deepest sentiments of Amish life.

RELIGIOUS RHYTHMS

Worship services held every other Sunday in their homes reaffirm the moral order of Amish life. As many as 200 or more persons, including relatives from other districts who have an "off Sunday," gather for worship. They meet in a farmhouse, the basement of a newer home, or in a shop or barn—underscoring the integration of worship and daily life. A fellowship meal at noon and informal visiting follow the three-hour morning service.

The plain and simple service revolves around congregational singing and two sermons. Without the aid of organs, offerings, candles, crosses, robes, or flowers, members yield themselves to God in the spirit of humility. The congregation sings from the *Ausbund*, a collection of German hymns without musical notations compiled by sixteenth-century Anabaptists. The tunes, passed across the generations by memory, are sung in unison without any musical accompaniment. The slow, chant-like cadence creates a sixteenth-century mood as a single song may stretch over 20 minutes.

Extemporaneous sermons, preached in the Pennsylvania German dialect, recount biblical stories as well as lessons from farm life as preachers exhort members to be obedient to Amish ways.

Communion services, held each autumn and spring, frame the religious year. These ritual high points emphasize self-examination and spiritual rejuvenation. Sins are confessed and members reaffirm their vows to uphold the Ordnung. The six- to eight-hour communion service includes preaching, a light meal during the service, and the commemoration of Christ's death with bread and wine. Near the conclusion of the service members pair off and wash each others' feet as the congregation sings. As members depart they give an alms offering to the deacon—marking the only time that offerings are collected in Amish services.

The baptismal service serves as the entrance to membership in Amish society. Baptism typically occurs between the ages of 16 and 22. Prior to baptism the candidates are instructed in the 18 articles of faith from the Dordrecht Confession of Faith, an old Anabaptist creed written in the Netherlands in 1632. Baptism is a pivotal moment in the life of Amish youth which signifies a confession of Christian faith and also a promise to obey the Ordnung of the church forever. Reflecting the voluntarism of their Anabaptist heritage, the Amish respect the integrity of individual decision. Those who reject baptism and drift away from the community without being baptized are able to continue fellowshipping with family and friends without the stigma of shunning. However, those who accept baptism and later renege on their vows face excommunication and social avoidance.

Worship, communion, and baptism are sacred rites that revitalize and preserve the Ordnung. The Amish, like other human beings, forget, rebel, experiment, and stray into deviance. Major transgressions are confessed publicly in a members' meeting following the worship service. Violations of the Ordnung—using a tractor in the field, posing for a television camera, flying on a commercial airline, filing a lawsuit, joining a political organization, or opening a questionable business—may require confession. Public confession of sin diminishes self-will, reminds members of the supreme value of submission, restores the wayward into the community of faith, and underscores the lines of faithfulness which encircle the community.

The headstrong who spurn the advice of elders and refuse to confess their sin will face excommunication. The exiles also encounter shunning, a cultural equivalent of solitary confinement. Members are expected to end social interaction with the wayward souls. A bishop compared shunning to "the last dose of medicine that you give a sinner. It either works for life or death…but if love is lost, God's lost, too." For the unrepentant, social avoidance becomes a lifetime quarantine. One excommunicated member noted, "It works a little bit like an electric fence around a pasture."

Shunning is a silent deterrent that encourages those who consider breaking their baptismal vows to ponder the consequences. This practice is used to preserve the purity of the church and encourage repentance. Excommunicated members, even years later, can be restored into membership upon public confession of their sins.

EDUCATION

"We're not opposed to education," said one Amish man, "we're just against education higher than our heads; I mean education that we don't need." Indeed the Amish had participated in public education as long as it revolved around one-room schools. Under local control, small rural

schools posed little threat to Amish values. The massive consolidation of public schools, however, sparked clashes between the Amish and government officials in the middle of the twentieth century. Confrontations in several states led to arrests and brief stints in jail.

After many legal skirmishes, the U.S. Supreme Court legitimated the eighth-grade Amish school system in 1972 in the landmark case of Wisconsin v. Yoder. In the words of the Court, "There can be no assumption that today's majority is 'right' and the Amish and others are 'wrong'." The justices concluded that "a way of life that is odd or even erratic but interferes with no rights or interests of others is not to be condemned because it is different."[9]

Today the Amish operate more than 935 parochial schools for some 25,000 Amish children.[10] Many of the schools are one-room operations with 25 to 35 pupils and one teacher who teaches all eight grades. A few Amish children attend rural public schools in some states but the vast majority

8. Most Amish children attend classes in a one-room schoolhouse built on land donated by a farmer in their district. They are educated up to an eighth-grade level, receiving instruction similar to that which is offered in public schools.

Photograph by Susan Einstein, Elkhart-LaGrange Counties, Indiana, 1981-1984

study in parochial schools governed by the Amish. A local board of three to five fathers organizes the school, hires a teacher, approves the curriculum, oversees the budget, and supervises maintenance. Teachers receive about $25 to $35 per day. The annual cost per child is roughly $250— nearly 16 times lower than many public schools, where per pupil costs often top $4,000. After funding the costs of their own schools, Amish parents also pay public school taxes.

A scripture reading and prayer open each school day, but religion is not formally taught in the school, or in other Amish settings for that matter. The curriculum includes reading, arithmetic, spelling, grammar, penmanship, history, and some geography. Classes are conducted in English and both English and German are taught. Parents want children to learn to read German so they can understand religious writings, many of which are recorded in formal German. Science and sex education are missing in the curriculum as are other typical trappings of public schools—sports, dances, cafeterias, clubs, bands, choruses, computers, television, guidance counselors, principals, strikes, and college recruiters.

Amish teachers, educated in Amish schools, are not required to be certified by most states. The brightest and best of Amish scholars, they return to the classroom to teach, often in their late teens and early twenties. Amish school directors select them for their ability to teach and for their commitment to Amish values. Teachers manage some 30 pupils across eight grades, without the benefit of high school or college diplomas. Periodic meetings with other teachers, a monthly teachers' magazine, *The Blackboard Bulletin*, and ample common sense prepare them for the task. Some textbooks are recycled from public schools while others are produced by Amish publishers.

Students receive a remarkable amount of personal attention despite a teacher's responsibility for eight grades. The ethos of the classroom accents cooperative activity, obedience, respect, diligence, kindness, and the natural world. Little attention is given to independent thinking and critical analysis—the esteemed values of public education. Despite the emphasis on order, playful pranks and giggles are commonplace. Schoolyard play during daily recesses often involves softball and other homespun games.

Amish schools are unquestionably provincial by modern standards. Yet in a humane fashion they ably prepare Amish youth for meaningful lives in Amish society. Parochial schools help to preserve Amish culture by reinforcing Amish values and shielding youth from alien ideas afloat in modern culture. Moreover, schools restrict friendships with non-Amish peers and impede the flow of Amish youth into higher education and professional life. Islands of provincialism, the schools promote practical skills that prepare their graduates for success in Amish society.

SOCIAL GATHERINGS

Various social gatherings bring members together for times of fellowship and fun beyond the biweekly worship. Young people gather in homes for Sunday evening singings. Married couples sometimes meet with old friends to sing for "shut-ins" and the elderly in their homes. Various frolics blend work and play together in Amish life. Parents often gather for work frolics in August to prepare a school building for fall classes. End-of-school picnics also bring parents and students together for an afternoon of food and games.

Quilting bees and barn raisings mix goodwill, levity, and hard work for young and old alike.

9 (OPPOSITE). Interior of an Amish schoolhouse.

Photograph by Susan Einstein, Elkhart-LaGrange Counties, Indiana, 1981-1984

Other moments of collective work—cleaning up after a fire, plowing for an ill neighbor, canning for a sick mother, threshing wheat, and filling a silo—often involve neighbors and extended families in episodes of charity, sweat, and fun. Adult sisters, sometimes numbering as many as five or six, often enjoy a "sisters' day," which blends laughter with cleaning, quilting, canning, or gardening.

Public auctions of farm equipment, held in February and March, attract crowds in preparation for springtime farming. Besides opportunities to buy equipment, the day-long auctions offer ample time for farm talk as well as gossip and friendly fun. Games of cornerball in a nearby field or barnyard often compete with the drama of the auction. Household auctions and horse sales provide other favorite times to socialize.

Family gatherings at religious holidays as well as summer family reunions link members into familial networks. Single women sometimes gather at a cabin or a home for a weekend of fun and frolic. Special meetings, often called "reunions," of persons with unique interests—harnessmakers, cabinetmakers, woodworkers, blacksmiths, businesswomen, teachers, and others—are increasingly common. A network of persons who have experienced bypass heart surgery circulates a letter in several states and holds an annual meeting. The disabled also hold an annual gathering. These various gatherings often attract persons from many different states.

Leisure and pleasure have long been suspect in Amish life. Idleness is viewed as the devil's workshop. In recent years the rise of cottage industries and more ready cash has encouraged more recreational activities. Said one Amish entrepreneur, "Some of us are businesspeople now, not just backwoods farmers, and sometimes we just need to get away from things."

Amish recreation, for the most part, is group oriented and tilts toward nature. Indeed, most forms of commercial entertainment are taboo. The Amish rarely take vacations but their "trips" to other settlements often include visits to scenic sites and state parks. Groups travel by chartered bus or van to other settlements for reunions, special gatherings, historical tours, or visits to a state park or public zoo.

Among youth, seasonal athletics—softball, sledding, skating, hockey, and swimming—are common. Volleyball is a widespread favorite. Fishing and hunting for small game are favorite sports on farms and woodlands. Some Amishmen in Pennsylvania own hunting cabins in the mountains where they gather in the late fall to hunt white-tailed deer. Deep-sea fishing trips are also common summertime jaunts for men living in East Coast settlements. Others prefer camping and canoeing. Pitching quoits is a typical activity at family reunions and picnics.

Some couples travel to Florida for several weeks over the winter. They live near Sarasota in an Amish village populated by winter travelers from several states. A trip to Mexico in search of special medical care may include scenic detours along the way. Although some Amish travel by train or bus, chartered vans are popular for distant treks. Traveling together with family, friends, and extended kin, members enjoy the laughter and chatter that builds the bonds of community.

HOLIDAYS AND FESTIVITIES

Cultural constraints shape the calendar of Amish holidays. As conscientious objectors, they have little enthusiasm for patriotic days with a military flair. Memorial Day, Veterans Day, and the Fourth of July are barely noticed; even Labor Day stirs little interest. The witches and goblins of

10. Public auctions, attended by both the Amish and the English, are usually held in the spring and fall.

Photograph by Susan Einstein,
Elkhart-LaGrange Counties, Indiana, 1981-1984

Halloween feel foreign to Amish spirits. Pumpkins may be displayed in some settlements, but without cut faces. Halloween parties are never held.

Amish holidays earmark the rhythm of the seasons and religious celebrations. A day for prayer and fasting precedes the October communion service in some communities. Fall weddings provide ample holidays of another sort. Persons without wedding invitations celebrate Thanksgiving day with turkey dinners and family gatherings. New Year's day is a quiet time for family gatherings. Some communities add a second day to their celebrations of Christmas, Easter, and Pentecost. The regular holiday is a sacred time that flows with quiet family activities. The following day (second Christmas, Easter Monday, and Pentecost Monday) offer time for recreation, visiting, and sometimes shopping. Ascension day, prior to Pentecost, is also a holiday for visiting, fishing, and other forms of recreation. "More visiting takes place on these springtime holidays," said one Amish man, "than at any other time."

Christmas and Easter festivities are generally spared commercial trappings. Families exchange Christmas cards and gifts. Some presents consist of homemade crafts and practical gifts, but increasingly many are store bought. Homes are decorated with greens but Christmas trees, stockings, special lights, Santa Claus, and mistletoe are missing. Although eggs are sometimes painted and children may be given a basket of candy, the Easter Bunny does not visit Amish homes. These sacred holidays revolve around religious customs, family gatherings, and quiet festivities rather than commercial trinkets and the sounds of worldly hubbub.

Birthdays are celebrated at home and school in quiet but pleasant ways, with cakes and gifts—but not at large-scale parties filled with clowns, balloons, and noisemakers. Parents often share a

11. The wedding table is elaborately set with lavish items rarely used in the Amish home: fancy china, cut glass, and ornamental floats of wood, macaroni, and flowers made by the wedding party.

Photograph by Susan Einstein,
Elkhart-LaGrange Counties, Indiana, 1981-1984

special snack of cookies or popsicles with school friends to honor a child's birthday. Birthday celebrations and other holiday festivities in the Amish world reaffirm religious roots, strengthen family ties, and underscore the lines of separation with the larger culture.

The wedding season is a festive time in Amish life. Young persons typically marry in their late teens or early twenties. Coming on the heels of the harvest, weddings are typically held on Tuesdays and Thursdays from late October through early December. The larger communities may have as many as 150 weddings in one season with a dozen or so on one day. Typically staged at the home of the bride, these joyous events attract upward of 350 guests. The three-hour service begins shortly after eight o'clock in the morning and is followed by a noon meal, singing, snacks, visiting, an evening meal, and festivities into the night. The specific practices vary somewhat from settlement to settlement.[11]

ARTISTIC RESERVATIONS

Amish culture has historically eschewed artistic expression. Several strands of their religious heritage have tended to stifle the artistic spirit. As descendants of the Anabaptist movement they often disdained the images and art of "high" Protestant and Catholic churches. Germinating over the years these sentiments sometimes even viewed works of art as vain idolatry—equivalents of biblically forbidden graven images.

Moreover, the individualistic streak in artistic expression collides with the communal values of Amish culture. Art that exalts the individual is disdained. Hung or displayed, personal portraits call attention to the individual and the artist. In the Amish mind, such expression breeds pride and arrogance. Historically, Amish-made dolls typically had no faces in order to avoid the appearance of a graven image and to erase individual expression. Photographs of individuals have long been forbidden in Amish culture for fear that they would cultivate conceit and thus encourage individualism. Most photos of Amish persons which appear in print are taken without consent with telephoto lenses in public settings.

Amish culture is rooted in the soil of practical rural values. Art, in Amish eyes, is an impractical and unnecessary frivolity. To rural peasants eking out a living by the sweat of their brow, art is a waste of time. Pragmatic and useful activities are treasured in Amish culture, not the fantasies of individual artists. Abstract art, with its multitude of interpretations, intrigues the modern mind, but the Amish want to know if something works—is it practical and useful? Congealing together, these cultural sentiments almost sealed the fate of Amish art.

The destiny of Amish art was not completely doomed, however. Expressions of folk art have bubbled out of Amish life over the centuries. Barbara Ebersole (1864-1922) was widely known for her fraktur—lovely artistic lettering. She was likely permitted greater artistic freedom because she was a dwarf. Ebersole designed colorful book plates for Bibles and other family records. Her designs of fancy hearts, tulips, and assorted flowers today top $3,000 at public auctions. Embroidered family registers, calendars, and genealogical charts have long decorated Amish walls. Lovely quilts, flower gardens, and homemade crafts are other age-old forms of artistic expression in Amish life.

In recent years the usefulness of Amish art has grown. Pushed off the land and greeted by millions of tourists, craft sales are soaring. Art has suddenly become useful—practical for making a living in the face of diminishing farmland. A wide spectrum of artistic expression has blossomed into crafts of all sorts but, all things considered, it still remains folk art. Saws, shingles, metal disks, and other domestic tools are cleaned and hand painted for sale. Needlework, corn husk dolls, and quilts are just a few of the hundreds of items produced and sold by the Amish.

One Amish artist complained about the church's view when she noted, "It's okay to paint milk cans but not to display your work at art shows." Even that is changing now. Some self-trained Amish artists are beginning to paint on canvas as well as to display and sell their work. One Amish artist was featured in *USA Today* in 1991. A first-time exhibit of Amish art appeared in Lancaster, Pennsylvania in 1991. Church leaders have permitted such ventures, especially for members with financial needs and when the art clearly involves "making a living" rather than displaying vain glories.

The new artistic expressions remain entrapped, however, by cultural norms. The pastoral scenes on canvas are limited to depictions of actual Amish settings. Individuals are rarely drawn. And when they are, faces are never shown. Although it appears on canvas and is designed to be hung and enjoyed, the new Amish art remains practical, still hemmed in by cultural values—surely not abstract expressions of post-modern imaginations.

OCCUPATIONAL CHANGE

Amish life is rooted in the soil. Ever since European persecution pushed them into rural areas the Amish have been tillers of the soil. The land has nurtured their common life and robust families. "It's been a long-standing tradition," said one leader, "that Amish families live on the farm, attached closely to the soil, and a good father provides a farm for his boys." In the words of

another leader, "Good soil makes a strong church where we can live together, worship together, and work together." Until recently the bulk of Amish families were farmers.

Amish attachments to the soil began to unravel in the middle of the twentieth century. The rising cost of farmland, suburbanization, tourism, and the growth of the Amish population have all contributed to the decline of farming. Land prices soared as urbanization devoured prime acreage. Farmland, for example, in Lancaster County, Pennsylvania, sold for $300 an acre in 1940. In the nineties the same land cost $8,000 to $10,000 an acre. If sold for development, the prices often doubled or tripled. Changes in agricultural technology and government regulations, especially those related to milk production, have made it difficult for some Amish farmers to earn a living. All of these factors, including their own rapid growth, have nudged Amish families off of the farm, particularly in the older settlements in Indiana, Ohio, and Pennsylvania.

In smaller settlements in more isolated areas, most Amish families continue to farm. The exodus from the farm has been steady in the past 30 years in the communities located near urban areas. In the Elkhart-LaGrange settlement of Indiana, the number of farmers dropped from 61 percent to 35 percent between 1970 and 1988. Many of them began working in recreational vehicle factories owned by outsiders. Indeed 45 percent of the household heads were employed in factories by 1988.[12] The Amish settlement in the Elkhart-LaGrange area is distinctive for its large number of factory employees.

The number of farmers in the Amish settlement in Geauga and Trumbull Counties in northeastern Ohio had already dipped to 30 percent by 1977. Today only 16 percent of the families in that area are engaged in farming. The remainder work in factories, shops, construction, logging, and sawmills.[13] Farming has also dwindled in the large Amish settlement in the Holmes County region of Ohio. In 1965 about 72 percent of household heads were farming but today only about 43 percent are tilling the soil.[14] Those who have abandoned their plows are involved in hundreds of small microenterprises as well as in factory work. A recent inventory lists over 700 Amish owned and operated microenterprises in the Holmes County area.

A similar pattern has emerged in Pennsylvania's Lancaster settlement. As early as 1977 the number of men farming had dipped to about two-thirds, but in recent years only about 50 percent have been plowing for a living. Unlike some other settlements, Lancaster has few persons working in factories. Those who have left the farm have established hundreds of cottage industries and small businesses. A recent investigation found nearly 1,000 Amish-owned microenterprises in the Lancaster settlement.[15]

The rise of cottage industries and small shops marks a sharp turn in Amish life. Mushrooming since the 1970s, these new enterprises are reshaping Amish ways. Amish retail shops sell dry goods, furniture, shoes, hardware, and wholesale foods. Church members now work as carpenters, manufacturers, mechanics, plumbers, painters, and self-trained accountants. Professionals—lawyers, physicians, and veterinarians—are, of course, missing from Amish ranks because of the taboo on higher education.

Despite the recent occupational changes few, if any, Amish are unemployed, and they rarely receive government benefits. The rise of cottage industries may, however, disturb the equality of Amish life in the long run by encouraging a three-tiered society of farmers, entrepreneurs, and day

12 (OPPOSITE). Interior of an Amish bedroom.

Photograph by Susan Einstein, Elkhart-LaGrange Counties, Indiana, 1981-1984

13. Most Amish farms are comprised of a large complex of buildings, including barns and silos for storage, a generous farmhouse for the large Amish families, and a separate "grandpa" house for the grandparents.

Photograph by Susan Einstein,
Elkhart-LaGrange Counties, Indiana, 1981-1984

laborers. Will prosperous shop owners turn their profits back to the community or spend them on lavish lifestyles? Parents worry that youth, working a 40-hour week with loose cash to spare, will snub the traditional values of simplicity and frugality. The new industries also encourage interaction with outsiders. Indeed, Marc Olshan has argued that Amish enterprises constitute the "opening of Amish society" because they not only welcome but legitimate interaction with the outside world that they have been taught to fear for more than three centuries.[16]

These rather dramatic occupational changes will surely transform the character of Amish life and culture over the generations. The rise of cottage industries and small businesses is an attempt by the Amish to preserve many of their traditional values. Nevertheless, the exodus from the farm will undoubtedly impact family size, revise child-rearing practices, alter attitudes toward work and leisure, increase interaction with the outside world, and introduce greater variations of wealth and status. It promises, in short, to be the most consequential change to touch the Amish community in the last half of the twentieth century.

POLITICAL ENTANGLEMENTS

The Amish view government with ambiguous eyes.[17] Although they support and respect civil authority, they also keep a healthy distance from it. On the one hand, the Amish follow biblical admonitions to obey and pray for rulers and encourage members to be law-abiding citizens. On the other hand, government epitomizes worldly culture and the use of force. The European persecutors of the Anabaptists were often government officials. Moreover, when push comes to shove, governments engage in warfare, use capital punishment, and impose their will with raw coercion. Believing that such coercion and violence mocks the nonresistant spirit of Jesus, the Amish reject the use of force, including litigation. Because they regulate many of their own affairs the Amish have less need for outside supervision.

When civil law and religious conscience collide, the Amish will sometimes take a stand and "obey God rather than man," even if it brings imprisonment. They have clashed with government officials over a variety of issues including education, midwifery, Social Security, workers' compensation, "slow-moving vehicle" signs, land use, sanitation, zoning regulations, health care, and wearing hard hats at construction sites, to name a few of many issues. Conscientious objectors, Amish youth have received farm deferments or served in alternative service projects during times of military draft.[18]

The church forbids membership in political organizations and public office holding for several reasons. First, running for office is viewed as arrogant, out of character with humility and modesty. Second, office holding violates the religious principle of separation from the world. Finally, public officials must be prepared to use legal force if necessary to settle civic disputes. The exercise of such force, to Amish thinking, mocks the meek stance of nonresistant values.

Voting is viewed as a personal matter; however, few persons vote. Those who go to the polls are likely to be younger businessmen concerned about local issues. Although voting is considered a personal matter, jury duty is forbidden. Joining political parties, attending political conventions, and campaigning for candidates flies in the face of Amish virtues—simplicity, humility, and separation from the world.

The Amish pay their fair share of taxes. In company with other Americans they pay federal and state income taxes, sales taxes, real estate taxes, and personal property taxes. Indeed they pay school taxes twice—for both public and parochial schools. Scant use of motor vehicles results, of course, in fewer gasoline taxes. Following biblical injunctions the Amish pay all levied taxes except Social Security, from which they are exempt. In some states they are exempt from workers' compensation and unemployment insurance.

The Amish view Social Security as a national insurance program rather than a tax. Congressional legislation in 1965 exempted self-employed Amish people from Social Security. In 1988 after years of discussion, Congress also exempted Amish people employed by co-ethnics. However, Amish employees in non-Amish businesses do not qualify for the exemption and must pay Social Security without reaping its benefits. Thus, most church members neither pay into nor tap Social Security. Bypassing Social Security not only severs the Amish from old-age pension payments, but it also closes the spigot to Medicare and Medicaid.

Government subsidies, or what the Amish call "handouts," have been stridently opposed. The Amish object to government aid for several reasons. The church, they contend, should assume responsibility for the social welfare of its own members. The aged, infirm, senile, disabled, and retarded are cared for, whenever possible, within extended family networks. To turn the care of these folks over to the state would abdicate a fundamental tenet of faith—the care of one's brothers and sisters in the church. Furthermore, federal aid in the form of Social Security or Medicare would erode dependency on the church and undercut programs of mutual aid which the Amish have organized to help members burdened by fire and storm damage as well as onerous medical expenses.

The prosperity that the Amish have enjoyed in the twentieth century can be partially attributed to the tolerable, or perhaps more accurately, accommodating political conditions which they have enjoyed in North America. Some of them have been arrested and indeed have sat in prison, but all things considered, they have fared rather well. In contrast to the sad fate of their religious forebears in Europe, none have been executed for their faith and few have chosen to migrate for religious reasons. Indeed, the ironies of history have brought tourists by the millions to gawk and gaze at Amish ways in some of the larger settlements. So in a strange twist of fate, those who were once hunted down and burned at the stake have become objects of public curiosity if not outright admiration and respect.

TECHNOLOGY

Popular images construe the Amish as organic farmers who milk their cows by hand and cook their food over an open hearth. The social facts, however, spoil this caricature of Amish life. The Amish do prefer the ways of nature, but they also accept some modern technology. A wide array of technology aids their work and enhances their comfort in kitchens, barns, and shops. Technology is selectively used and sometimes limited or harnessed in special ways.

Progressive Amish homemakers typically use, among dozens of other common household items, spray starch, detergents, instant pudding, disposable diapers, Ziploc™ bags, and permanent press fabrics. Modern bathrooms, the latest gas appliances, and air powered tools are common in some Amish settlements. Families in the more conservative communities still use outhouses and do not have refrigerators. Except for a few battery-powered gadgets, electrical appliances and lights are missing from Amish homes. Televisions, computers, and radios, of course, are taboo. Moreover, electric dryers, blow dryers, microwaves, air conditioners, and other electrical appliances, of course, are not used. Washing machines are often powered by gasoline engines, hydraulic pressure, or air pressure. Water is often heated by gas. Homes are normally heated by kerosene or coal heaters or, in some cases, by wood stoves.

In the more progressive settlements a wide array of technology—automatic milkers, tractors, elevators, welders, and electric cow trainers which are powered by batteries—supports farming operations. The more conservative churches do not permit automatic milkers or the use of bulk tanks for cooling milk. In many settlements pesticides, insecticides, preservatives, and chemical fertilizers are widely used alongside modern veterinary practices. Although frowned upon historically, artificial insemination of dairy cattle is being used in some states. But there are limits; embryo transplants are taboo. Silo unloaders, milk pipelines, milking parlors, automatic barn cleaners, self-propelled equipment, and field tractors have not received the blessing of the church in even the most progressive Old Order communities.[19]

Shops and cottage industries employ a vast array of mechanical equipment, albeit powered by hydraulic and air pressure. Some craftsmen work with plastic and fiberglass materials. Small 12-volt motors, electrical inverters, and diesel engines energize shop equipment in the more progressive settlements. Electronic cash registers, digital scales, and electric calculators, powered by electrical inverters hooked to batteries, are commonplace in these communities as well. But again, some limits lace this world. Computers and standard electrical equipment—with a few exceptions—are

14 (OPPOSITE). A modern Amish home reflects the values and restraints of Amish life. The kitchen appears quite modern but in fact does not use any electricity; all power in the home is generated with gas, kerosene fuel, or battery-operated devices.

Photograph by Susan Einstein, Elkhart-LaGrange Counties, Indiana, 1981-1984

15. The barn raising is a communal event. Approximately 100 men build a barn in only a few days while the women provide the food and the children carry out any necessary chores.

Photograph by Susan Einstein, Elkhart-LaGrange Counties, Indiana, 1981-1984

forbidden. Some mobile carpentry crews may use electrical tools at construction sites, but not at home.

Despite popular misconceptions, the Amish are not a fossilized relic of the past. Economic pressures prodded by farming and microenterprises have spawned many changes. Other changes have come as families sought ease, comfort, and convenience within the boundaries of Amish society. Innovations which pose little threat to Amish identity or community solidarity are usually overlooked. Gas grills, for example, have appeared on Amish patios in recent years. Instant coffee, disposable diapers, and chain saws have been welcomed by many Amish groups while in other cases, ordained leaders have drawn firm lines. Computers are generally banned because leaders fear they would lead to video games and television.

PATTERNS OF SOCIAL CHANGE

The Ordnung, as interpreted by church leaders, regulates the rate of social change. Once embedded into the Ordnung, taboos are difficult to overturn. Sometimes new technology is accepted on top of old taboos, yielding a perplexing riddle. Several examples illustrate this baffling pattern of social change. Power lawn mowers were forbidden in the 1950s in some settlements for fear that they would spawn ostentatious lawns and proud hearts, and steal work from Amish youth. A decade later farmers were permitted to mount engines on field mowers. Still later, "weed eaters" powered by small gasoline engines were deemed appropriate for lawns and gardens. Yet the taboo on power lawn mowers held firm across the years. Thus, today, some homesteads sport old-fashioned push mowers alongside modern weed eaters and large power mowers in the fields.

Telephones and cars illustrate a similar pattern. Telephones were first barred from homes in the early decades of the twentieth century. Later they were permitted at the end of lanes and eventually adjacent to barns and shops and finally inside shops in some progressive church districts. However, the original taboo on home phones held firm. While trying to respect the initial taboo, church leaders yielded to pressures for phones for business purposes which brought a zigzag pattern of telephone use. So although generally banned from homes, phones are found in various places outside the home depending on the views of the local bishop.

A ragged pattern of change has also followed the car. The original proscription against ownership has held, although leaders have gradually permitted widespread hiring of vehicles to accommodate the growing need for mobility. The church has made a sharp distinction between ownership and use of motor vehicles. Members may not own or operate vehicles, but they may rent taxi service for business purposes and long distance trips. The extent to which vehicles are used varies widely from settlement to settlement.

Practices which might erode traditional taboos or bring cultural contamination—microwave ovens, television, video games, video cameras, and computers—have little chance of being accepted by the church. Other practices and products which pose no threat—trampolines, hot dogs, and battery-powered calculators—slip into place with little fuss. A patchwork pattern of social change often results as elders try to retain traditional practices while also nodding to pressures for new technology. Moreover, what is permitted varies considerably from settlement to settlement and rests somewhat on the disposition of the local bishop. Working together, the bishops in the same affiliation try to uphold the basic markers of Amish identity as prescribed by the Ordnung. Each bishop, however, is permitted some latitude of interpretation and application.

The lines of discretion which restrict the use of technology are drawn from many sources. Many of the prohibitions are tied to the religious principle of separation from the world. Some of the limits flow from fears that large farms and shops will disrupt the order and equality of community life. Other restrictions are designed to stymie the cultural contamination which might come via computers and televisions. The taboo on owning motor vehicles and using tractors in fields is designed to limit mobility and encourage family-related work which binds the community together and impedes social fragmentation. Still other guidelines rest on symbolic taboos—holding firm over the years—which preserve Amish identity. The selective use of technology by the Amish helps to reinforce community solidarity and arrest assimilation into American culture.

THE AMISH ENIGMA

The growth of this unique community creates an enigma of sorts. Why are the tradition-laden Amish not merely surviving but actually flourishing in the midst of modernity? How is it that people who shun high school, television, air travel, the use of computers, and the ownership of automobiles are not withering away but are, indeed, thriving? By what means are the Amish able to spurn the temptations of modernity rather than fade into oblivion? Political toleration and their esteem as a cultural icon of sorts have surely enhanced Amish growth and vitality. Yet these are not enough. Other unusual groups who enjoy similar religious freedoms have not necessarily flourished like the Amish.

Their robust growth rate is produced by sizable families and the retention of most of their off-spring. The Amish do not engage in missionary activities. A few outsiders occasionally become members, despite the wide cultural gap. The typical family has six or seven children on average, but some families have ten or more. Throughout the twentieth century the Amish gradually began using modern medicines and the services of physicians and trained midwives. These practices have reduced infant mortality and encouraged families to flourish. Children are an economic asset in an agrarian economy. In Amish eyes they are also viewed as blessings from the Lord.

Although no official statements prohibit artificial birth control, the Amish have discouraged such tampering with divinely ordained means of reproduction. There is growing evidence, however, that some Amish couples, especially younger ones living off the farm, are limiting the size of their families by natural and artificial means. It remains to be seen if Amish families will shrink in size as more of them enter nonfarm occupations. In any event the robust size of Amish families, at least in the past, has provided a large pool of recruits for membership.

Large families do not necessarily produce growth; children must be persuaded to join the community. What attracts youth to the church and what compels members to remain? Retention rates vary by settlement and affiliation and also fluctuate with economic, social, and religious circumstances. In the three largest settlements about 80 percent or more of Amish offspring remain with the church. Some 81 percent of young adults affiliate with the church in the Elkhart-LaGrange settlement in northern Indiana. The Lancaster settlement retains at least 90 percent of its youth. In the Holmes County area of Ohio the Old Order Amish persuade more than 85 percent of their youth to stay with the church.[20]

Numerous practices encourage Amish youth to join and remain in the ethnic community. The social and financial security provided by a stable community is attractive. The church has maintained visible symbols of ethnic identity, particularly clothing, which mark clear-cut lines of separation from the world. Interaction with the larger culture is bridled by taboos on motor vehicles, television, radio, and higher education. However, the church has not been rigid; it has been willing to accept technological changes which enable members to sustain a comfortable standard of living. The rise of Amish schools since mid-century has helped to preserve Amish ways and cultivate a distinct sense of identity. All of these factors explain the enigma of Amish society—how a tradition-oriented group manages to flourish in the midst of modernity.

What of the future of Amish life? Projections for twenty-first-century Amish life elude easy forecast, but one trend is clear. Settlements pressed by urbanization are the most progressive in outlook and the most likely to accept modern technology. In short, they are the most willing to negotiate with modernity. Rural enclaves beyond the tentacles of urban sprawl remain the best place to preserve traditional Amish ways. If the Amish can educate and retain their children, make a living without merchandising their souls, and restrain interaction with the larger world, they will likely continue to flourish in the twenty-first century. But one thing is certain: diversity between settlements will surely grow and continue to mock the staid stereotypes of Amish life.

NOTES

1. Dyck (1993) provides a general introduction to the rise of Anabaptism and Mennonite-Amish history. The five-volume *Mennonite Encyclopedia* provides excellent resources for information on Anabaptist history and present-day groups.

2. For a general introduction to Amish history consult Nolt (1992). Roth (1993) has recently translated the letters surrounding the Amish division of 1693 and reviews the issues involved in the controversy. Hostetler (1993) provides a general introduction to Amish life and culture and Kraybill (1989) traces social changes in the twentieth century in the Amish settlement in Lancaster, Pennsylvania. Kraybill and Olshan (1994) explore *The Amish Struggle with Modernity* in Amish communities across North America. A more popular introduction to Amish life with color photographs can be found in Kraybill and Niemeyer (1993).

3. Yoder (1991) chronicles the issues that provoked controversy in the Amish communities in the last half of the nineteenth century and subsequent formation of the Old Order groups. See also chapters 8 and 9 of Nolt (1992) and the work of Beulah Stauffer Hostetler (1992:5-25) for a comparative analysis of Old Order origins.

4. A listing of all the Amish settlements in North America by state and province was compiled by Luthy (1994). This enumeration includes the founding date and number of congregations in the settlement.

5. This estimate is based on the assumption that church districts average about 150 persons (children and adults). The number is higher in the older settlements such as those in Lancaster County, Pennsylvania, and Holmes County, Ohio, and somewhat lower in the small and newer settlements. Thus 150 is a reasonable estimate for all settlements. At the beginning of 1993 there were approximately 930 church districts in North America with an estimated population of 140,000. These numbers are based on Luthy's (1994) listing of settlements.

6. This is the number of settlements that were established and still in existence at the end of 1992. About 18 additional settlements were founded but failed during these two decades according to Luthy's (1994) calculations.

7. Olshan and Schmidt (1994) discuss the conundrums of gender roles in Amish society in the context of feminist theory.

8. The history and work of The National Amish Steering Committee are described by Olshan (1993 and 1994a).

9. The full text of the Supreme Court's decision as well as several essays discussing the case are available in Keim (1975).

10. Meyers (1993) and Huntington (1994) provide good historical overviews of the rise of Amish schools and the various conflicts with the state. Hostetler and Huntington (1992) describe the cultural ethos and curriculum of Amish schools.

11. For descriptions of wedding practices in various Amish communities, consult Scott (1988).

12. These figures appear in Meyers' (1994) detailed study of occupational changes in the Elkhart-LaGrange settlement.

13. Peter Gail reports the current number in various occupations in this settlement in an article in the April 1994 issue of the Plain Communities Business Exchange.

14. Kraybill (1994) discusses the occupational shifts and social change in the Holmes County region of Ohio, the largest Amish settlement.

15. The dramatic rise of these microenterprises in Lancaster's Amish community is described in detail in a full-length book by Kraybill and Nolt (1995).

16. The impact and long-term consequence of these enterprises on Amish society is discussed more fully in Olshan (1994b) and Kraybill and Nolt (1994 and 1995).

17. For an in-depth discussion of the Amish view of the state, see Yoder (1993).

18. A series of essays edited by Kraybill (1993) describes in depth the conflicts between the Amish and the state over many of these issues.

19. A few Old Order communities in Iowa and Kansas and many New Order groups use tractors for field work. Most Old Order churches forbid the use of tractors in the field but permit their use for high-power purposes around the barn.

20. In a recent article, Meyers (1994) reports his findings of defection patterns in the Elkhart-LaGrange settlement. He found retention rates ranging from 68 to 92 percent between 1920 and 1969. The estimate of 81 percent for the Elkhart-LaGrange settlement is based on data compiled in the *Indiana Amish Directory, LaGrange and Elkhart Counties, 1988*. The estimates for the Lancaster, Pennsylvania settlement are based on a study of 20 church districts conducted in 1986 by Kraybill (1989:14). The sources for the Holmes County, Ohio settlement are found in Kraybill (1994).

Quilts within the Amish Culture

Patricia T. Herr

OPPOSITE: Detail of CAT. 21

"Clear and warm. We had a quilting Today: Sarah and Rebecca, Susie Bare, Fannie, & Rebecca & Lizzie & Lizzie Fisher were here. They finished it." Susan S. Lapp of Ronks Post Office, Lancaster County, Pennsylvania, entered these words into her diary on Tuesday, 8 June 1886.[1] Information from diaries and personal interviews with contemporary Amish women indicate that quilting and quilt making activities have been an important part of home textile production and the social structure of Amish women from the later nineteenth century to the current time.

LANCASTER COUNTY QUILTS

The Lancaster County Old Order Amish community seems an apt paradigm for the study of the social and economic context of quilts in Amish culture. This area of southeastern Pennsylvania was, in fact, the location of the first Amish settlers in the New World. It contains highly productive farmland within easy reach of major markets, so the Amish settlements in the Lancaster region grew, prospered, and became a central point from which families migrated to other destinations in North America (Deeben 1990). With this prosperity in such a close-knit community came the opportunity to develop highly sophisticated crafts with a specific regional style.

By the second quarter of the twentieth century, members of the sect had begun to feel the encroachment of other cultural groups, a loss of productive farmland, and the advent of tourism in Lancaster County. In response to these pressures, the Amish made conscious decisions to become involved with commercial endeavors not directly related to farming and agriculture (Kraybill and Olshan 1994:113-81). Within the Old Order Amish community of Lancaster County is evidence that as early as the 1860s women were creating a highly sophisticated and specific form of quilted bed cover for their own use.[2] In doing so they were fulfilling an important social function within the framework of the feminine component of the community. But before a century had passed, Amish women were responding to the external pressures by using their talents to produce quilts for sale to the outside world. The trend has now grown to become what one reporter calls "Lancaster County's Fastest Growing Home Industry" (Klimuska 1987). To explore this quilt tradition in depth we need to look back to the first European Amish settlers in the New World and examine their textile heritage.

SWISS ORIGINS

17 (OPPOSITE, LEFT). Coverlet, hand woven, wool and cotton with center seam in Star and Diamond patterned multiple shaft weave structure, dated "1836" and initialed "A+K," dimensions 246.4 x 198 cm. The initials and family history suggest this coverlet was made for 16-year-old Anna Kurtz, an Old Order Amish woman, before her marriage to Jacob Stoltzfus. This is the earliest known surviving Amish bed covering and is typical of coverlets used by other Pennsylvania German settlers living in the Lancaster County area.

Private collection

A few Amish families may have arrived with the Swiss Mennonites in 1710 and settled in Pequea, in the southern end of Lancaster County. But the bulk of eighteenth-century Amish immigrants, estimated to be about 500 persons, arrived in Pennsylvania between 1737 and 1754. These people settled in the Berks, Lebanon, and Lancaster County areas of southeastern Pennsylvania and also were primarily of Swiss origin. Later nineteenth-century migrations of Amish, probably totaling about 3,000 persons from various parts of the European continent, settled in other areas of the United States (Hostetler 1993:55–65). So the textile traditions of the Lancaster County Amish stem mainly from Switzerland.

BED COVERINGS BEFORE QUILTS

Because of the small number of Amish settlers among the colonists, few examples of eighteenth-century Lancaster County Amish textiles survive. With knowledge of these few early surviving pieces, as well as descriptions in eighteenth-century Amish letters and account books, we may assume that Amish textiles of this period did not differ significantly from other Anabaptist Pennsylvania German settlers' belongings that survived in larger numbers.

The primary bed covering used by the Pennsylvania German colonist was the handwoven coverlet, which would have lain over the plaid linen tick cover that surrounded the feather tick (Keyser 1978) (FIG. 16). The earliest such documented Amish bed covering is the wool and cotton, handwoven, multiple-shaft, Star and Diamond patterned coverlet seen in Figure 17. This piece has cross-stitched in the lower right corner "A+K 1836." According to family history and genealogy, it belonged to Anna Kurtz, an Old Order Amish woman who would have been 16 years old in 1836 (Gingrich and Kreider 1986). This particular coverlet, which does not differ significantly from other handwoven Lancaster Pennsylvania German bed coverings of the period, almost certainly was woven by a professional weaver from the Lancaster County area near where the Kurtz family lived.

There are several journals, pattern books, and account books of Amish professional weavers who worked in Lancaster County during the eighteenth and nineteenth centuries making coverlets and producing yardage for clothing, bedding, and household use.[3] Such records indicate that they were producing textiles for Amish and non-Amish neighbors. The Amish also could have purchased

16. A Pennsylvania German bed dressed as it might have been ca. 1800. Handwoven coverlets were in common use at this time by the Germanic immigrants in Pennsylvania.

2 FEATHER PILLOWS
FEATHER BOLSTER
STRAW BOLSTER
COVERLET
FEATHER BED
BED SHEET
CHAFF BAG

woven goods from some of the many non-Amish professional men weaving in the immediate area. But because these were all products of male professional weavers, it is not likely that bed coverings of this period were designed at home.

Although Jacquard patterned coverlets were becoming popular with non-Amish members of the community in the late 1830s, there is no evidence to suggest that the Amish in Lancaster County were buying them at this time. However, the Old Order Amish of Lancaster County were purchasing Jacquard patterned coverlets in the latter part of the nineteenth century, after many other Pennsylvania Germans had abandoned their use. Factory woven coverlets, those made in shops containing several looms and weaving large numbers of unsigned, undated bed covers, often appear among the textile belongings at Amish house sales. The blue and white example in Figure 18 was probably locally manufactured between 1870 and 1900. The Amish seemed to have favored blue or purple and white combinations. An entry from an Amish woman's diary of 1892 supports this use of coverlets as she notes: "I patched pants and hemed [sic] a cover lid [sic]."[4]

INTRODUCTION OF QUILTING

The earliest quilts thought to be made by Lancaster County Amish women, and thus the first home-manufactured bed coverings used in the Amish community, seem to be whole-cloth glazed

18 (ABOVE, RIGHT). Coverlet, Jacquard patterned, wool and cotton, late nineteenth century, probably manufactured in the Lancaster area, dimensions 210 x 193 cm. This type was used by the Lancaster Amish long after others had abandoned the coverlet as a common bed covering. The Amish preferred two-color coverlets, usually blue or purple and white.

Collection of Nailor Antiques

19. Quilt, Whole Cloth pattern, Quaker, plain-weave silk top, linen quilting thread, plain-weave cotton back, wool batting, dated "1752," dimensions 251.4 x 255 cm. This quilt, made by Quaker Hannah Trotter, who married Jeramiah Elfreth of Philadelphia, represents the earliest type of quilt found in the Pennsylvania-Delaware Valley area. Some similarities in quilting patterns and designs are shared by Delaware Valley Quaker and Lancaster County Amish quilts. Typical of eighteenth-century Quaker quilts, Hannah's piece is quilted with linen thread and filled with wool batting. This differs from the nineteenth-century Amish quilts included in the following illustrations, all of which have cotton quilting thread, batting, and plain-weave cotton backs.

Collection of Elfreth's Alley Association

cotton and wool covers like the example in Figure 20. Although the fabric of the top surface of this piece does not allow for a pattern definition, the quilting does. A border has been defined by the use of a wide band of cable stitching, with a circular star or floral motif delineating the corner blocks. This example is dated and initialed "1869 G.D." It was purchased from an Indiana Amish family but is thought to have originated in Lancaster County. Another similar example found in a Lancaster Amish family is marked "1868 J.D."[5] The introduction of quilting activities into the Old Order Amish household sets the stage for the development of a unique cultural form, the Lancaster County Amish quilt.

Evidence from inventories and quilts found in this area of southeastern Pennsylvania would suggest that the quilting tradition was introduced by the English colonists who settled side by side with the Pennsylvania Germans. Indeed, in many ways the eighteenth-century whole cloth silk and wool Quaker quilts from neighboring Chester and Philadelphia counties resemble the early Lancaster County Amish quilts (FIG. 19).

DEVELOPMENT OF THE LANCASTER QUILT

No longer dependent on the outside manufacture of patterned bed coverings, the local community and family group could choose and influence directly the quality, content, color, and patterns of their bed coverings. Who made these decisions, and why, merits further research and reflection. Using the artifacts and archival materials presently available, we have much to learn about the development and production of the quilt within the confines of such a close-knit and socially isolated society as the Old Order Amish Lancaster community of the late nineteenth and early twentieth centuries.

What appears to be the next step in the development of the Lancaster Amish quilt is the bed cover dated "1875" and bearing the initials "G.D." illustrated in Figure 21. Known to collectors as the Center Square, its simple pattern is also found in other Amish communities in North America. In this example we see the use of the Quaker feather motif in the border quilting. It closely resembles the feather designs in Quaker Hannah Trotter's quilt, and it would become a popular border quilting pattern in use well into the twentieth century in Lancaster Amish bed coverings. The quilting patterns in the plain central area of this example are laid out in block motifs, suggesting the pieced block centers that didn't come into use until the 1920s in Lancaster County.

Although not many documented examples of quilts made from 1880 to 1900 survive, it is clear from diary entries written by Amish women during this period that quilting was an important part of Amish home life. The craft was not limited to the manufacture of bed coverings. Entries in 26-year-old Barbara L.

Stoltzfus' 1892 diary describe making the following items: Wednesday, 20 January, "I put a settee cushion in the frame to quilt"; Saturday, 26 November, "Sister Babbie was along & Nancy we quilted a peticoat [sic]"; Wednesday, 7 December, "Today it was cloudy & I quilted [a] bonnet one for me & one for Sarah [her daughter]."[6]

WOMEN'S WORK ROLES

Quilting was but one part of textile production that took place in the home. Textile related activities were only a portion of the many responsibilities of an Amish woman in maintaining the household. Diaries from 1885 to the current time quite precisely describe the daily household duties of various members of the family.

Besides what we might consider the normal household chores of cooking, cleaning, child care, washing and ironing, and shopping, women were responsible for the planting, harvesting, and upkeep of the yard, and flower and kitchen gardens (FIG. 22), not to mention the resulting canning and preserving of food. In the early years, before the shipping of milk off the farm, they also were responsible for making the butter, which often was sold as a cash crop. In the twentieth century, it appears from diaries that poultry production was often the women's responsibility. That would include not only gathering and marketing the eggs but also caring for and feeding the birds and cleaning the hen houses.

In the cold weather, when outside work was slow, the whole family, including women and children, worked together shelling corn and stripping tobacco to prepare it for sale. Again, at the peak

20 (ABOVE, LEFT). Quilt, Whole Cloth, Amish, glazed plain-weave cotton and wool top, cotton quilting thread, cotton back, cotton batting, dated "1869" and initialed "G.D." Although found in Indiana, this quilt has a Lancaster County provenance and represents what is probably the earliest type of quilt to have been made by Lancaster County Amish women.

Indiana State Museum Pottinger Collection

21 (ABOVE, RIGHT). Quilt, Center Square pattern, Amish, dated "1875" and initialed "G.D.," wool top, cotton quilting thread, cotton back, cotton batting, dimensions 208 x 208 cm. The Center Square is thought to be one of the earliest Lancaster Amish patterns. This example, along with the plain quilt shown in Figure 20, is among the earliest dated Lancaster Amish quilts known.

Private collection

22. Postcard, Old Order Amish woman working in her garden in Lancaster County, Pa. Gardening, the production of food for the family and for sale at roadside and market stands, is traditionally the responsibility of women in the Amish household. Most Amish gardens also boast a bumper crop of colorful flowers. The importance of garden produce to the economic health of the Amish family is one reason women have a high status within Amish society. Published by Stel-Mar, Lancaster, Pa.

Collection of Jim Ward

23 (OPPOSITE). Socks and mittens, Amish, hand-knit, wool, late nineteenth century. Amish diaries from the 1880s indicate that a great deal of time was spent knitting such items to clothe family members. By the early twentieth century, commercially knitted clothing was considered acceptable for use by the Amish community in Lancaster County.

Private collection

of planting and harvesting, the women and children could be found in the fields working on tobacco and other field crops in addition to their daily household chores.

TEXTILE PRODUCTION IN THE HOME

A significant amount of household work time was devoted to household textile production from the mid-1880s through the 1950s, a period for which diaries are available. It should be remembered that the Old Order Amish, for the most part, still produce their own clothing from purchased yard goods. Although they have commercial sources for towels, bedding, shoes, hats, knitted hosiery, and underwear, sewing is still a time-consuming activity. But with the introduction and acceptance of synthetic fabrics, particularly polyesters which Amish women have wholeheartedly embraced, the lifetime of the individual garment has been greatly extended. The use of these fabrics cuts down not only on fabrication time but also time spent on washing and ironing. Figures 25-28 illustrate four periods in which representative women's diaries were analyzed for the mention of household textile manufacture. The activities recorded fall into five major areas: knitting (FIG. 23), quilting, rag carpet preparation (FIG. 30), rugging (hooked and braided rug making) (FIG. 29), and sewing (FIG. 24).

One can see that throughout this period, the two consistent textile production activities were sewing and quilting. As might be expected, more time was spent on general textile production during the earlier periods than in recent times. The great amount of time spent on knitting in 1886 was not necessary after the Amish adapted to using commercially made hosiery, mittens, and sweaters. Although rag carpets are still used in some contemporary Amish homes, the number of Amish weavers producing hand-loomed carpet has considerably diminished. On the other hand, rug hooking seems to have become popular with Lancaster Amish women only in the early twentieth century, and by mid-century it was phasing out. The braiding of rugs seems to have been done in the latter part of this period, and to a lesser extent than hooking. Surviving examples of these various textile forms in family possession and public and private collections support this diary information.

It is evident that such activities varied considerably with the age of the diary keeper. There is the potential for a great deal of information to be gathered from diaries about fabric production throughout the various life stages of an individual Amish woman.

In reading Amish diaries, one is also struck by the cyclic nature of activities necessitated by close ties to the land and the need for women to spend concentrated time gardening. Early spring is planting time and in early summer the produce must be picked and preserved. One Amish quilt maker born in 1927 remembers the rhythm of the seasons in this way:

> Quiltings were usually held after the spring work was finished.... There was always a wonderful meal made. You never took a dish.... Quiltings were mostly held when you had fresh garden food.... When the lettuce, radishes, peas, potatoes were ready, early June and in early fall maybe.... Too hot to sit around and quilt. July, August it's harvest time....[and] fall silo filling is too busy.[7]

Although sewing and, in the nineteenth century, knitting activities were necessary all year long to maintain clothing supplies, activities such as quilting and rugging could be planned on a more sporadic basis when time would allow. A peak time for sewing and quilting tended to be in the late summer and early fall to make school clothes for the children and prepare quilts for the October wedding season.

THE SOCIAL ASPECT OF TEXTILE PRODUCTION

Frequently, textile-making activities would become social functions. The actual quilting of a bed cover after it was in the frame called for a gathering of friends, relatives, and neighbor women. The piecing and preparing of the back, filling, and binding would be readied for a time when a number of women would gather and finish the quilting within the day. In diaries of women who seemed to be particularly active quilters, like Susan S. Lapp, a 22-year-old who was keeping a diary in 1886,[8] quilting sometimes involved just family members and was done on a number of successive days until the quilt was out of the frame.

It is interesting to note that when Susan mentions the location of a quilting, it is usually described as being at "Christ Glicks," "Henry Fishers," or "Samuel Fishers," not at the home of the

24. Baby dress, Amish, wool and velvet with cotton lining, 1895, length 78.7 cm, sleeve length 12.2 cm, waist 24.1 cm. This dress was made by Sarah Lapp Smoker for her daughter Elizabeth, born in 1895. It was probably a special dress made for Elizabeth's first visit to church. Amish clothing of this period was hand-made except for specialty items such as shoes, hats, and bonnets. Nowadays, most Lancaster Amish purchase manu-factured socks and underwear and make their outer garments of longer-lasting synthetic fibers, thus reducing home sewing time.

Collection of Kathryn and Daniel McCauley

AMISH HOME TEXTILE PRODUCTION

Figures 25 through 28 show the five major types of home textile production mentioned in Amish women's diaries written between 1886 and 1958. Although textile activities varied from family to family and emphasis differed among the diarists according to age and interest, the diaries represented here are typical of the many read and analyzed by the author. Of the five textile activities—quilting, rug hooking, knitting, sewing, and rag carpet preparation—two seem to persist as important home activities throughout the period under consideration. They are quilting and sewing. Interviews conducted with contemporary Amish women by the author indicate this is still true in today's Amish home.

25 (RIGHT, ABOVE). In 1886 Susan Lapp occupied many of her quiet moments with sewing and knitting. Although some of this was done in her own home, a considerable amount of her sewing and knitting activities occurred when she was working as a hired woman for various relatives. The same can be said for rag carpet preparation. This activity entailed cutting, sewing together, and rolling into balls strips of fabric, which would then be sent to a professional carpet weaver to be made into strip carpeting. There were no comments about rug hooking found in Amish diaries of the late 1800s, and the author knows of no Lancaster County Amish hooked rugs made during this period. Susan did quite a bit of piecing and quilting at home as well as quilting with her unmarried friends. She also mentions quiltings her mother held or attended with other older married women.

1886 SUSAN S. LAPP DIARY
FIGURE 25

unmarried 22 year old woman

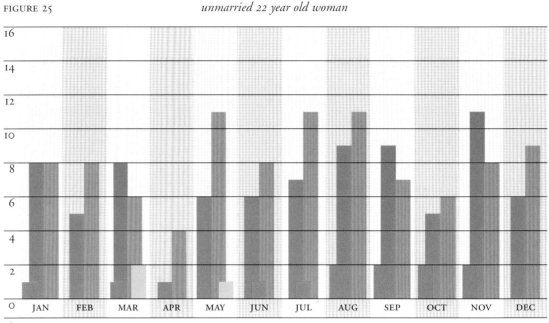

NUMBER OF ACTIVE DAYS PER MONTH

1922 MARY M. BEILER DIARY
FIGURE 26

unmarried 16 year old woman

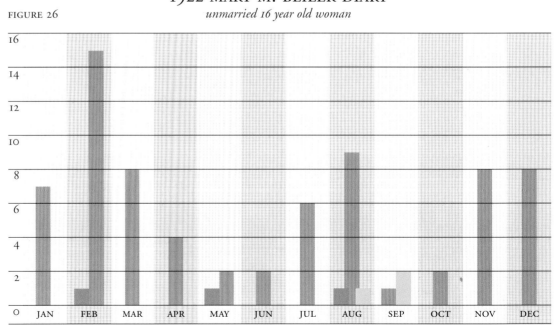

NUMBER OF ACTIVE DAYS PER MONTH

TEXTILE PRODUCTION ACTIVITIES

QUILTING   RUGGING (HOOKED)   KNITTING   SEWING   RAG CARPET PREP.

1938 ANNIE S. STOLTZFUS DIARY

FIGURE 27   *unmarried 17 year old woman*

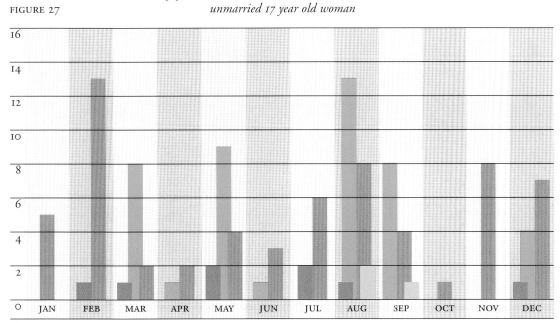

▲ NUMBER OF ACTIVE DAYS PER MONTH

1958 ANNIE S. STOLTZFUS DIARY

FIGURE 28   *unmarried 37 year old woman*

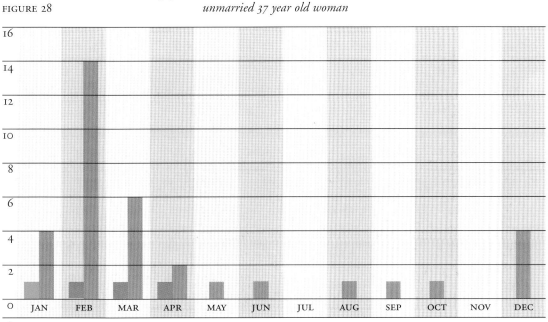

▲ NUMBER OF ACTIVE DAYS PER MONTH

26 (OPPOSITE, BELOW). In Mary M. Beiler's 1922 diary there is no notation of knitting activities in her home. Undoubtedly, commercially produced stockings, socks, caps, and sweaters had replaced the hand-knit products. In the Beiler family, rag carpet preparation and quilting persisted, but sewing seemed to be the most popular textile production activity. Mary makes no mention of quilting at home, but she and her mother did attend quiltings with their respective friends.

27 (LEFT, ABOVE). Annie S. Stoltzfus frequently mentions her rug hooking in her 1938 diary. Indeed, many Amish hooked rugs from this era survive in Lancaster County. The 17-year-old girl seemed to enjoy this pastime at "the rugin," as she calls it, as well as working on her rug frame at home. Within this family, "rugins" seemed to supplant quiltings as women's social gatherings. However, both Annie and her mother participated in quiltings and rag carpet preparation.

28 (LEFT, BELOW). The same Annie S. Stoltzfus, still unmarried and living at home in 1958, provides diary information for the latest period in the analysis. She and her mother still did some rug hooking by themselves at home in the late 1950s. They occasionally quilted at a relative's, but the bulk of their textile production time was spent sewing. No knitting or rag carpet activities are described.

29 (ABOVE). Hooked rug, Amish,
wool on burlap, ca. 1940, dimensions
58.4 x 106.7 cm. This pattern of a team
of horses surrounded by pansies has
been executed in several variations by
Lancaster County Amish women. Note
that in this rendition there appear to be
only six legs between the two horses.

Private collection

30 (RIGHT). Rag carpet, Amish, cotton
rag weft, cotton warp, handwoven,
warp-faced, plain-weave, early twentieth
century, dimensions 442 x 91.4 cm.
The professional carpet weaver used rags
prepared by the Amish women. His
carpet loom was hand operated and he
provided the cotton yarn for the warp.

Private collection

Glick or Fisher women. Susan's diary entry for Monday, 8 February 1886, which reads, "Lydia [her sister] and I went over to Leah Fisher['s,] were quilting[,] had a fine time," likely refers to her neighbor Leah Petersheim Fisher, widow of Jonathan L. Fisher (Committee of Fisher Descendants 1988). So although these activities were decidedly feminine in nature, they occurred within the framework of a patriarchal society. As with normal daily conversation among the Amish, the diarists seldom wrote about personal feelings or noted any value judgments they may have made about people or situations described. So it is somewhat uncharacteristic for Susan to have written, "had a fine time."

A postcard sent in 1926 by Susie Zook of Gordonville, Lancaster County to her 20-year-old friend Susie Reno of Route #3 in New Holland leaves no doubt that these were planned social events. Susie's penny postcard reads:

Dear Friend a few lines in a hurry. I am having a quilting on Tuesday May 26. You can come if you want to if you don't want to come by yourself get Ida Stoltzfus or Mary King to come along. I wrote both of them this morning. I must close this. From Susie Zook. Be sure and come.[9]

More than just a social event, quiltings had special significance to the Amish women in the community. In the words of Miriam Stoltzfus, remembering her days as a young Amish woman:

Quilts said a lot to the community. If you were busy quilting this said you were going to get married. It was an honor to be invited to a quilting because [as a young girl] that would give you self-confidence, you're able to quilt now. You wanted to be a good quilter. You would just not miss a quilting![10]

She goes on to say that quilting was an art to which every girl was exposed and that it was a must to piece and to learn how to quilt. In her family she, as the oldest girl, was responsible for making her brothers' quilts. Among her friends, most started piecing at about 13 years of age when they finished school. By 16 years of age they could look forward to being asked to a quilting.

Even Lancaster Amish women weren't immune to the newest fads; as a 1978 nine-cent postcard to Mrs. Emanuel Fisher suggests, other pastimes in the twentieth century joined quilting as a communal activity. Her brief penciled message states: "A Stanley Party at James' Stoltzfoos Mon. March 6[,] 7:30 P.M. come bring a friend."[11,12]

When hooked rug making was popular among Lancaster Amish women, this activity sometimes became a social event in the manner of quilting. Annie S. Stoltzfus in her 1938 account of daily life writes on Saturday, 5 March 1938, "I was at Uncle Sam's Lapp's at the rugin. Our crowd was at Sammy's Dan's over night." And on Tuesday, 24 May 1938, she wrote, "I was at the rugin at David Smucker's. And Mother was quilting there. In the evening we ruged at home." On Tuesday, 2 August of the same year, Annie records, "I was rugin at Uncle Aaron Esh'es. Aunt Lydia, Aunt Priscilla, Uncle John's Katie and Annie Lapp and Uncle John's Annie went up in the morning and came home in the evening[.] Christ King[']s Levina and Rebecca were there too." Again on Thursday, 4 August 1938, she entered, "Mother and I were at Uncle Mose Zooks' to help rug and sew." However, the majority of "rugin" that Annie records she did at home on her own. This contrasts with her quilting activities, which always involved her or her mother being invited with others to a quilting.[13]

Lancaster Amish quilts made over a span of almost 100 years are relatively consistent and homogeneous, yet they differ significantly from quilts of other Amish settlements. Investigating the methods of fabric and pattern choice will help the reader understand this recognizable group of bed coverings and their variations, and how these came about.

QUILT FABRICS

The sources of fabrics available to Amish women have always been varied.[14] They include local stores owned by Amish and English[15] merchants, mail order catalogs, and traveling salesmen. The ca.-1923 postcard illustrated in Figure 31 is a view of downtown Lancaster; it shows an Amish woman and child out on a shopping day, walking by a clothing store advertisement. Note the trolleys and horse-drawn buggy in the background. Well into the 1960s, the major Lancaster department stores had plainclothes sections catering to the local conservative sects, primarily Old Order Mennonite, Amish, and Brethren. With trolley, horse-drawn buggy, and, later, bus transportation available, they were not limited to hometown fabric purchase. Mail order houses like Sears Roebuck advertised plain goods for the plain sects and were as near as the mailbox at the end of the farm lane. Traveling salesmen came right to the door. It is from interviews with these salesmen and their families that one can begin to gain an understanding of how and why the fabric choices were made.

One of the major traveling salesmen firms, or peddlers, as they were known in Amish communities throughout the country, was the Sam J. Greenberg Co. of Philadelphia (see Figure 32, showing an advertisement proclaiming, "Plain Goods for Plain People"). Interviews with Sam's son Bill and granddaughter Joyce Brown,[16] both of whom were known to the Amish during their respective tenures as "Sam Greenberg," reveal how they loaded up the car or station wagon with yard goods purchased from merchants in New York and Philadelphia and traveled the circuit of Amish settlements from the easternmost point in Lancaster to Indiana. The Greenbergs and other Jewish peddlers, including Sam's brother Nathan, who dealt mainly with the team Mennonites,[17] and cousin Isaac Korsch provided many of the fabrics used in Lancaster Amish quilts from the 1920s through the 1960s. Joyce Brown still maintains a dry goods supply store in Intercourse. The peddlers' arrival was eagerly anticipated by woman and children alike. The children would swarm over the bolts of yard goods looking for some new or appealing fabric, trinket, or gift. "Sam" was always careful to show each new type of material to the bishop of that church district for approval before peddling it to the quilters and seamstresses of the region. What he brought depended in large part on special deals that he could make with fabric wholesalers in the city and quality fabric choices that he knew were consistent with the values held by the various Amish communities he visited. Each community across the country had different needs and values, which he took into consideration when buying. If a fabric did not seem to have an appealing name, he often would invent one to differentiate his from the competition. The Amish had their own names for fabric, some of which Greenberg coined; "Robinette" was named after his granddaughter Robin and "Pettijohn" for grandsons Peter and John.

31. Postcard ca. 1923 showing an Amish woman and child walking along North Queen Street in the downtown shopping area of Lancaster City. On the right beyond the L. Weber & Son jewelry store window is a sign stating, "DRESS FOR ENTIRE FAMILY HEAD TO FOOT $1.00 PER WEEK." Amish families were frequent customers in the city for fabrics, some manufactured clothing, and other household and dry goods. They found it easy to ride in on a trolley car or a horse and buggy, both of which can be seen at the left side of the photograph.

Private collection

The Morgantown quilt maker reminisces about the times when a salesman came to the house to sell fabrics in the early 1940s:

A lot of times there's people that came out of Philadelphia,…which were the Jews. [They] would bring a carload of fabric to your door. That was mainly how my mother got her best materials. They learned exactly what the Amish wanted…. And they'd give you a good deal because you took a large quantity.

I would say twice a year…when I was a teenager we looked forward because I would need a new dress. We knew it meant new dress material, we were so eager…. It was always plain, never a print. He opened up his trunk, all standing around. That was typical of every home in the neighborhood of all the Amish people. He would cover a whole area within a couple days. And that was the talk of the next Sunday with us girls. What did each one get?

And Romaine crepe! That was a fabric! It started to come in when I was a teenager. And whoever had a Romaine crepe dress that following season, man, they were top, on top of the mountain! Oh, everybody had Romaine crepe. It came in such beautiful colors.[18]

The subtle choices of fabric for clothing and quilts among the Lancaster County Amish reflect a great deal about the individual's status within the community. The same quilt maker elaborates on these subtleties:

> Your quilt reflected a lot on you, if your quilts had expensive material. Batiste[19] was the Cadillac material. The men that wore batiste suits…and what the ladies called [their] suits. You arc much put in catcgorics by thc way you keep your house, by the kind of material, the kind of stitches you do in your sewing. The width of the strings on the covering was a big deal. If they were way wide you were really Amish, the narrow ones you were getting uppity.[20]

Clothing and quilt fabrics were primarily commercially dyed and woven cotton, wool, or silk and wool combinations of plain or twill-weave. Some rare examples of glazed plain-weave cotton top quilts survive as possibly the earliest Lancaster County examples (see the earlier section, Introduction of Quilting). As rayons became commercially available in the 1930s, they too were adapted to quilt and clothing manufacture. Amish women have since accepted the introduction of other synthetic yarns such as nylon, polyester, and acrylics. The use of weave patterned or printed patterned materials has been limited to quilt backing. These types of fabrics are seldom found in a quilt top. Even today this use of patterned and printed materials would be unusual among the Lancaster County Old Order Amish in making quilts for their own use.

The Morgantown quilt maker explains the practicality of fabric choice when she was a girl in the early 1940s.

> [About the best quilt] It is very fine stitching…10 stitches to the inch…and it is batiste. And of course the colors are dark, and they always chose [sic] dark because you would never wash it. You would just hang it up, air them out.
>
> The quilts that you made for your everyday bed, which was the everyday quilt, were made out of material that you could wash. But also dark, largely dark, because it didn't show the dirt.[21]

QUILT PATTERNS

Quilt pattern choices were determined in much the same way. Subtle differences may be seen within specific families within a church district. But, for the most part, the community pressure to maintain boundaries within which members functioned limited the Lancaster County Amish women's choice of quilt patterns to a few selections. These patterns are noticeably different from those of other Amish communities within Pennsylvania and other more western settlements. Therefore, the quilt connoisseur is able to easily identify the typical Lancaster patterns of the Center Square, Center Diamond, Sunshine and Shadow, and Bars. It is, however, the recognition of subtle differences that illustrates the tension of the balance between conformity and innovation within Amish life.[22] Donald Kraybill (in this volume) eloquently describes this balance in his discussion of the *Ordnung* or unwritten code of conduct.

"Did people come up with patterns that weren't like anybody else's?" When asked this question,

32. Early twentieth-century advertisement of the Sam J. Greenberg Co. of Philadelphia, an enterprise started by Sam in the 1920s and continued by his son William and now granddaughter Joyce. The family members all have been known to Lancaster Amish women simply as "Sam Greenberg," the Jewish peddler who comes to the house with a station wagon piled high with fabrics. Philadelphia Jewish merchants were a major source of Amish clothing and quilting fabrics in the early twentieth century.

33. Sunshine and Shadow pattern quilt, Amish, wool and cotton top, cotton quilting thread, cotton back, cotton battings, made between 1925 and 1930, dimensions 218.4 x 218.4 cm. Rachel Beiler's rendition of the Sunshine and Shadow quilt with an added inner sawtooth border is different from most others of this pattern. The author knows of only two other sawtooth variants of the design, and they also had belonged to Beiler family members.

Private collection

the Morgantown quilt maker, who left the Amish faith after her marriage, replied:

> Yes, they did, the more progressive ones that allowed their minds to think. They'd come up with something new, but normally your mind is pretty well geared to think on what has already been done. Well why change? Their [the Amish] statement has been…, "It was good enough for our parents and it's good enough for us." Or they would say, "We have good hope for our parents or for our grandparents and that's a hope we want." When someone dies you hear that so much, "We had good hope for them, why don't we follow in their foot-steps? They have gone to heaven, they have that good hope. Now let's study their life." When anyone wants to overstep some of their rules and regulations they will bring that out. "Now what would your grandparents think? Now this is going against your mother [and] father.[23]

VARIATIONS WITHIN BOUNDARIES

The quilt shown in Figure 33, made by Rachel Beiler in the 1920s for her own use, is a variant of the Sunshine and Shadow pattern in which the maker has inserted an inner sawtooth border. The author has seen only two other such quilts, both belonging to the Beiler family. Other Sunshine and Shadow quilts, one of the most common patterns made by Lancaster Amish women, seem to vary from the basic formula only in the presence or lack of corner blocks.

Another general variation seen in Lancaster Amish quilts in the choice of a block pattern instead of an overall central motif as found in the Bars, Sunshine and Shadow, Center Diamond, and Center Square patterns. Although block patterns are the typical choice of Amish quilt makers in the Midwest, they are far less common in Lancaster-made quilts. The most likely block patterns to be seen in Lancaster quilts are the Nine Patch, Crazy Block, Fan, and Baskets. In each case these seem to be the production of a small group of family and neighborhood friends.

The two quilts illustrated in Figures 34 and 35 show the Baskets pattern. Except for color choice and small variations in the quilting motifs, these quilts are quite similar. The example in Figure 34 was made for Daniel Lapp, probably by his mother, Mary Stoltzfus Lapp. Another strikingly similar quilt, in a private collection, dated and initialed "1926 M.L.," is also attributed to Mary Stoltzfus Lapp. The quilt seen in Figure 35 was made by Sarah Stoltzfus for her brother Samuel. Sarah remembers making five quilts at that time. (Including Samuel, Sarah had four siblings.) Her mother, who did not enjoy quilting, chose the pattern for two of the quilts from a Baskets patterned quilt seen at her friend Katie Smoker Glick's home. Sarah then copied Katie Smoker Glick's pattern on cardboard, selected the fabrics from local stores in Intercourse and New Holland, and made two Baskets patterned quilts, one for her brother Samuel and one for herself.[24]

Katie Smoker Glick was a close relative of Mary Stoltzfus Lapp, the maker of the earliest known of these bed coverings. So it is not hard to understand how this particular pattern was transferred. Currently known are only six of these Lancaster Amish Baskets quilts.[25] They are all traceable to this small group of women and are strikingly similar in pattern, fabric choice, and quilting. Although the Baskets pattern is commonly used in other Amish settlements, these rare Lancaster examples are distinctly different from the Midwestern variety.

The practice of making quilts for all the children, both boys and girls, before marriage was standard among Amish families. Thus, as we see with the Lapp, Glick, and Stoltzfus quilts, they could have been made by mothers for their children or by another more talented woman quilt maker in the family. The number of quilts each child received seemed to depend on how much quilt-making activity took place in that particular family.

COMMERCIALIZATION OF QUILT MAKING

As discussed previously, outside pressures caused Lancaster Amish women to look at quilt production as a source of income for families not able to totally sustain themselves through agricultural activities. The postcard in Figure 36, produced sometime during the 1950s or 1960s,[26] shows what was probably the first Amish roadside stand to cater to tourists. The Moses B. Stoltzfoos family, or "Ice Cream Moses" as he was known, not only sold homemade ice cream and farm products but

34. Baskets pattern quilt, Amish, wool top, cotton quilting thread, cotton back, cotton batting, dated "1931" and initialed "D.L.," dimensions 200.1 x 203.2 cm, made for Daniel Lapp, probably by his mother, Mary Stoltzfus Lapp, four years before his marriage in 1934 to Lydia Smoker. This quilt represents one of the "first generation" Lancaster County Amish Baskets quilts. Mary's sister Barbara Stoltzfus Glick also made a quilt of the same pattern. Block design quilts were an uncommon choice of Amish women, and all of the known quilts of the Baskets pattern can be traced to a small family group living in Gap, a community in southeastern Lancaster County.

Collection of Jay and Susen Leary

also hung quilts out on a clothesline to attract the tourist to the Pennsylvania Dutch country.[27]

The quilts hanging on the Stoltzfoos clothesline—Log Cabin, Double Wedding Ring, and some appliquéed block patterns—are not typical of those an Amish woman would have produced for her own home at that time. These were being made specifically for the tourist. The Stoltzfoos family enterprise was an anomaly: the majority of the tourist quilt retail shops prior to the 1970s were owned by Mennonite women.

One Mennonite quilt maker, Emma Good of New Holland, owed her start in the busy retail quilt trade in the late 1950s to the Jewish fabric peddler from Philadelphia, Bill Greenberg.[28] He had long admired the color, design, and quality of the quilts being made by his customers, the Amish women in Lancaster County. So in the late 1950s he approached some of them about making a quantity of quilts, for which he supplied the fabric and paid the women $35 a quilt.

Greenberg, in turn, planned to market them in New York City. After this effort failed, he advertised the quilts in a Philadelphia newspaper at $75 apiece. As Greenberg tells it, "The phone was ringing off the hook." Women readers inundated him with stories about their quilt making days and memories of quilts in their families and childhood quilt stories. But no one bought a quilt!

At this point the peddler brought them back to Lancaster County and sold them to Mrs. Emma Good of New Holland, which, as Emma Witmer (Emma Good's daughter) relates, put her mother in business.[29] For some years she had been an avid quilt maker for her family and for sale. In 1959 the family had closed its roadside produce stand in front of the house. When Greenberg approached her with a large number of completed Amish-made quilts, she decided to open a shop. From that time on, she employed Amish and Mennonite neighbor women to make quilts to sell in her shop. This busy operation, Witmer Quilts, continues today at the same location and is owned by Mrs. Good's daughter, Emma Witmer.

Another local shop, one of the largest Amish-owned establishments in the Lancaster area, owes its start to Emma Good. When the would-be proprietor was about 11 years old, she contracted rheumatic fever and could no longer help with the field work. Her mother suggested that she make quilt patches, the embroidered type that the Amish placed in their light quilts (FIG. 37). She enjoyed the embroidery and, as was typical of Amish taste at the time, used a great deal of purple on white. Wanting to turn these efforts into cash, she took the patches to Emma Good to sell, but Good did not like the purple color, thinking it was not what the public would buy. This prompted the Amish girl, who lived in the village of Witmer near Bird in Hand, to set up her own shop. In 1972 she hung

35. Baskets pattern quilt, Amish, wool top, cotton quilting thread, cotton back, cotton batting, dimensions 208 x 208 cm, made by Sarah Stoltzfus for her brother Samuel in about 1939. Sarah's mother saw a Baskets quilt on a bed at Katie Smoker Glick's home. (Katie was Barbara Stoltzfus Glick's daughter-in-law.) Sarah's mother, who was not a quilter, liked this pattern and chose it for Sarah to make for all her siblings. In total, Sarah made five Baskets pattern quilts, similar in design and stitching, but of various color combinations. These quilts represent the "second generation" of Lancaster County Amish Baskets pattern quilts.

Private collection

up her sign and sold 30 quilts. The number quickly increased to 200 a year. Now she sells more than 500 a year and is assisted by her daughter in the business. This Amish quilt shop owner now pays a number of Amish and Mennonite women to make quilts for her.[30]

She started by accepting finished quilts brought in by local women, but now she buys the fabrics and patterns herself and provides them to her makers. That way she feels she can best meet the needs of her customers with more control over the type and quality of merchandise that passes through her shop. She also can get good prices on large quantities of fabrics from mail order houses and area fabric warehouses that have a sales force and home delivery. This shop owner is willing to work with an "English" customer who wants a quilt of a specific color or pattern and often does so, but she also has on hand a large selection of ready-made quilts to chose from or to use as a starting point for a special request.

Other Amish women making and selling quilts from their homes responded to the same economic and social pressures as the Bird in Hand shop owner. They were intrigued and curious about these outsiders who would pay $300 to $400 for a quilt. Some of them have raised their families and gotten out of other on-farm retail activities, like the Mennonite quilt maker, Emma Good. One Amish family that includes three generations on the same farm in Narvon, near the Lancaster-Chester County border, sells directly to Main Line Philadelphia women who come on Saturdays to select the pattern and fabric for their quilts. These women—a grandmother, her sister-in-law, and a granddaughter—all take part in the quilt making. The granddaughter has children at home and tends to spend less time with the business. The women do not keep quilts on hand but make them specifically for an individual order. Their business is totally word-of-mouth, as they do not have a sign or advertise in any other way. It would not be typical for an Amish woman to advertise her business in the newspaper or with printed cards or promotions, but many women are now marketing directly to the public. It is difficult to know what percentage of Amish women sell directly to the public and how many work for other quilt shops, but there is no denying that today more Amish women than ever are active quilt makers.[31]

This need to strengthen the economic condition of the rural Amish people at a time when less land was available revitalized the art of quilt making within the Lancaster Amish community. One woman who was raised Amish and whose grandmother and mother were excellent quilters learned the art from her mother in the 1950s. But when she came of age, little quilt-making activity was taking place within the family. Only after a boom of commercial quilting activity, to which her mother responded by establishing a quilt shop in about 1970, did she again take up the activity to help with the family business. Although this particular family has now left the Old Order Amish Church, they are representative of many Amish families from whom the craft of quilt making had all but disappeared.

The quilt makers who are working for the Witmer Amish woman are essentially doing piecework in their homes; they regard this as a business arrangement, not an opportunity for a social group quilting. The shop owner discourages group quilting as the work may vary too much in quality. Of course, she is able to pick her workers to obtain the most competent, reliable, and consistently good quilters, and there is competition within the Amish community for these particular quilters. They are wooed not only by the local Amish and Mennonite home quilt shops, but also by the myriad of commercial outlets that have sprung up in strips on the main streets of the local tourist towns of Bird in Hand and Intercourse. In a sense this is a paradox in the Amish culture, where group or community values have always been regarded as more important than those of the individual. For commercial purposes the group activity of quilting is regarded as of lesser value than the competent individual quilter's effort.

36. Postcard produced sometime in the 1950s or 1960s shows what may have been the first Lancaster County retail Amish outlet for quilts. The legend on the back of the card identifies the subject as "Mose B. Stoltzfoos 'Ice Cream Farm', in the Heart of The Dutch Country, E. Eby Road, Leola Road, #1, Pa. Serving homemade ice cream for thirty five years." The quilts visible on the clothesline are not patterns that would have been used by the Amish and may not have been Amish made. Published by Mt. Bethany Co. Creation, Ephrata, Pa.

Collection of the Lancaster Mennonite Historical Society

37. Ribbon pattern quilt, Amish, cotton top, cotton quilting and embroidery thread, cotton back and woven cotton cloth as interlining, dimensions 195 x 195 cm. Made for Hannah Beiler Stoltzfoos by women of the family in about 1954 before her marriage. This pattern is based on the traditional Center Diamond pattern so closely identified with the Lancaster County Amish quilting tradition. The traditional solid border sashes have been replaced by broken lines which resemble the 5 in-and-out weaving of a ribbon. The dark colored fields are now white and the quilting thread is of contrasting colors of embroidery floss with blanket and running stitches for added decoration. Hannah also received a "dark" quilt of the Sunshine and Shadows pattern as part of her dowry. Traditionally each child still receives a "dark" and a "light" quilt made and set aside for marriage. The dark one would still most likely be of the Sunshine and Shadows pattern, differing little from the traditional 1930s version. The light quilt is now more likely to be a block pattern quilt with the white blocks embroidered with floral motifs with the predominant colors being blue or purple. Present day quilts are made from polyester fabrics and batting for easy care.

Private collection

QUILTS IN THE AMISH HOME TODAY

Just as the quilts hanging on the shop clothesline of "Ice Cream Moses" back in the 1950s did not resemble the quilt he would have had on his own bed, the quilts that are sold from the Witmer Amish shop, made by Amish women, are not usually the same type that they would make for their family members. But Amish women still do make quilts for home use and for their children in preparation for marriage and setting up housekeeping. Traditionally, a girl will have ready before marriage a Sunshine and Shadow dark quilt (FIG. 33) and a pure white quilt. She also might have other light quilts prepared, such as the bed covering pictured in Figure 37. The background on these light quilts may be white or colored, but never off-white. There is still little use of prints, only occasionally in the light quilts, and little appliquéing is done for personal use. Traditionally, the fabrics incorporated in family quilts were the same materials used for clothing. In the last few years has emerged more of a tendency to buy specific fabrics just for quilts. The exposure to a larger variety of materials and patterns has no doubt affected the choice of quilts being made for use in the Amish home. The source of patterns has not varied much over the years. The Witmer shop owner uses handed-down patterns, ones obtained from swapping at quilting bees, and now patterns borrowed from other quilt shops.

Amish women in Lancaster County still participate in social quiltings when making quilts for their own use and to raise money for charity. Since most Amish families do not carry health insurance, the community often will be called upon to raise money for large medical bills; quilt sales, along with bake sales and community auctions, are an accepted way of doing this. Quilts still continue to be made as gifts. Typically, an Amish girl will invite her sisters, sisters-in-law, cousins, and friends to make a quilt for a soon-to-be married girl. This will be a gift and they want everyone to be involved in the gift-giving process.[31]

The Witmer Amish quilt shop owner feels that the women quilting for her for pay differentiate between that type of quilting and the quilting they do for family, friends, and community. Quilting for their own use gives them an opportunity to socialize and be part of a larger community group, whereas piecework at home, even though they enjoy the craft, is looked on in a different way, as an income-producing activity. She feels that if a quilt has been group-quilted, this should be told to the buyer.

This woman concedes that the quality of quilting has been dropping overall. That is not to say excellent quilters are not still plying their needles. With more people living off the farm, she explains, with a need for additional income, there are more Amish people than ever doing quilting, piecing, stamping, and binding. These are often jobs taken by older women whose children are raised. They can earn the money and stay at home.

According to this Amish quilt shop owner, the church bishops do not frown on the practice because the extra income helps pay the mortgage and may save the farm for an Amish family. Dr. John A. Hostetler (1993:363) comments succinctly on this issue: "Innovations that are accompanied by economic rewards have a greater chance of being accepted than do changes that are noneconomic in character."

This same shop owner feels that if booming quilt sales to tourists had been a factor earlier in the century, this would have made trouble for the Amish by keeping family members from their regular farm work. But now, as some seasoned observers of Amish culture like Hostetler and Stephen Scott (Klimuska 1987, Scott 1986) agree, commercial quilting activities may actually be a factor in preserving the Lancaster Amish community.

Has this ability to bring in extra cash income raised the status of Amish women in the society? Women always have had a position of importance within Amish society.[32] They, like non-Amish members of a farming family, are "partners in the production of the family livelihood," rather than

38. Postcard picturing the Amish farmers' curb market located by the old Lancaster Courthouse in downtown Lancaster, postmarked 1911. Here Amish families could sell produce and baked goods and bring in much-needed cash to the family farm. Amish women were an integral part of this activity.

Collection of the Lancaster Mennonite Historical Society

housekeepers for absentee husbands (Myers 1994:178). Another way of stating the importance of the Amish woman's position in her society is this statement made by Hostetler (1993:15): "Within her role as a homemaker she has a greater possibility of achieving status recognition than the suburban housewife; her skill, or lack of it, has direct bearing on her family's standard of living." When asked, a former Amish woman pointed out that Lancaster Amish women responded during the depression of the 1930s by making extra baked goods and raising more garden crops to sell at market in Lancaster City bringing much needed cash into the home.[33] Even before that, Amish women contributed significantly to the cash flow by producing goods for the sale at the old Amish curb market by the courthouse in downtown Lancaster (FIG. 38). The making of quilts and crafts for sale to the public, she feels, is not so different. It merely maintains the women's status within the community.

As for the place quilt making occupies in everyday modern Amish life, the Amish shop owner from Witmer says, "Quilting keeps their minds occupied; if quilting ever stops there will be a lot more people at the doctor's office."[34]

The Morgantown quilt maker also comments on the importance of quilts in Amish life:

> They took an awful lot of pride in the [quilt making]. That pretty well set the stage for which category you fall into, as far as ability and workmanship. It was very much a part of you, the quilt aspect. The kind of material, the stitching and of course the patterns, colors.

She remembers how she felt about quilts as a girl growing up in an Amish household:

> I had to do it, piece the quilts and see that it gets going, for my two brothers, because my mother was still having babies and doing other things. And more than that it was important that I learn, know it. And the only way that you learned was by doing. [After that] I had dropped it [quilt making]. After I had done what I needed to do at home for my brothers, I pieced a good many quilts. And the quilts that I then received from home I kind of decided I'd rather have chenille spreads and something else, because I was actually tired of these quilts.[35]

Commenting on her old dark quilt, one of those she received from her mother as a girl, which was put away in a chest and never used, this 68-year-old former Amish woman said, "I guess it has become more of a part of me than I realized."[36]

ACKNOWLEDGMENT

The author wishes to thank C. Eugene Moore for his editing skills, which enhanced and clarified this manuscript.

NOTES

1. Susan S. Lapp, diary, 8 June 1886, "Ronks P.O. Lancaster County Pennsylvania." Private collection. Susan was a 22-year-old unmarried woman in 1886.

   Both Amish men and women kept diaries, but more examples of women's diaries seem to have survived. Some were kept by schoolgirls as young as ten years of age and some diarists continued off and on throughout their lives. Many of the older diaries were kept by unmarried women. The majority of diaries are written in English although the language spoken within the Amish community is still primarily a German dialect. This is probably because the Amish learn to write English in school, but most Amish do not formally learn to write in dialect.

   The author wishes to thank Thomas Conrad and Thomas Wentzel for their insight and assistance in the study of Amish diaries and for making their collections of Amish material available for this purpose.

2. Orlofsky (1974) discusses Lancaster Amish quilts within the context of other quilts made in America. Bishop and Sanfanda (1976) and McCauley (1988) consider Lancaster Amish quilts as they relate to other American Amish quilts from a collector's point of view.

3. For an example of a published work, see Mast 1991.

4. Barbara L. Stoltzfus, diary, 26 April 1892. Barbara was a 26-year-old married woman living at Eby Post Office, Lancaster County, Pa.

5. The author wishes to thank Eve Wheatcroft Granick and David Wheatcroft for information about these early quilts.

6. Barbara L. Stoltzfus, diary, 1892.

7. Interview with a quilt maker from the Morgantown area by Patricia Keller, Quilt Harvest Data, collection of the Heritage Center Museum of Lancaster, Inc., 12 May 1990. This woman was born Amish in 1927. She and her husband left the church after their marriage in 1949.

8. Susan S. Lapp, diary, 1886, Lancaster County, Pa., private collection.

9. Postcard collection of the Lancaster Mennonite Historical Society, 2215 Millstream Rd. Lancaster, Pa. 17602.

10. Interview, Morgantown area quilt maker.

11. "Stanley Party" refers to the home marketing of Stanley kitchen products, similar to today's Tupperware parties.

12. Lancaster Mennonite Historical Society postcard collection.

13. Annie S. Stoltzfus, diary, 1938, Kirkwood, Pa., private collection. Annie was 17 years old in 1938.

14. For an in-depth discussion of sources of fabric for quilt making refer to Granick 1954:57-71.

15. This is the term the Amish use for non-Amish people.

16. Interviews with Bill Greenberg of Greenberg Co., Intercourse, Pa., 8 August 1992, by Patricia Keller and the author on the occasion of his 80th birthday party and at his home in Philadelphia, 3 September 1992, by Pat Keller, Quilt Harvest Data, collection of the Heritage Center Museum of Lancaster, Inc. The September interview is preserved on videotape.

17. A term used for the conservative Old Order Mennonites of the region who use horses and buggies and in many ways are hard for the outsider to differentiate from the Old Order Amish.

18. Interview, Morgantown area quilt maker.

19. Batiste is a term the Amish in Lancaster use for a high quality, finely woven, plain-weave wool fabric that was popular in the earlier part of the twentieth century for use in clothing and quilts.

20. Interview, Morgantown area quilt maker.

21. Ibid.

22. The reader might wish to review Hostetler's discussion (1993:300-06) of the modes of individual adaptation—conformity, ritualism, innovation, and retreatism—as they are found among the Amish.

23. Interview, Morgantown area quilt maker.

24. This information was gathered from personal interviews with the Gap, Pa. quilt maker and other family members done by Patricia Keller and the author on 28 January 1989, under the auspices of the Heritage Center Museum's Lancaster County Quilt Harvest.

25. Other quilts of this group are pictured in Granick (1989:76), Hughes and Silber (1990:pl. 77), and Holstein (1973: pl. 41). The images in the last two references appear to be of the same quilt.

26. Lancaster Mennonite Historical Society postcard collection. The author wishes to thank James Ward (Stevens, Pa.) for his expertise in locating and dating old Lancaster postcards.

27. The printed description on the back of this card states: "Mose B. Stoltzfoos—'Ice Cream Farm', in the Heart of the Dutch Country, E. Eby Road, Leola Road, #1, Pa. Serving homemade ice cream for 35 years. A must STOP for Dutch Country visitors."

28. Interview, William Greenberg.

29. Interview by telephone with Emma Witmer, Witmer Quilts, New Holland, Pa., 19 and 21 July 1995.

30. Interview with Amish quilt shop owner, Witmer, Pa., 16 May 1995.

31. Interview on audiotape with Louise Stoltzfus, editor for Good Books and interpreter of Amish life at The People's Place, Intercourse, Pa., by author, Quilt Harvest Data, collection of The Heritage Center Museum of Lancaster, Inc., 16 May 1995.

32. Sue Bender (1989) gives the reader an accurate account of the position of the contemporary Amish woman within her society.

33. Interview, Louise Stoltzfus.

34. Interview, Amish quilt shop owner.

35. Interview, Morgantown quilt maker.

36. Ibid.

In Plain Sight
The Aesthetics of Amish Quilts

Jonathan Holstein

Through the efforts of researchers around the world, a coherent history of quilts and quilt making is slowly emerging. One important area, however, remains stubbornly obscure. Unlike the study of many other designed or aesthetic works, in which we can often count upon a recorded art history and a system of research to help us discover their authors, quilts remain in large part anonymous, with all that implies in reducing the amount and richness of information we can derive from them. A small number of the whole are signed, or have associated documentation that reveals their makers. The authors of the vast majority are, and likely will remain, unknown to us.

We do a little better with broader demarcations. We know that almost all American quilts were made by women; we can assign to most of them a reasonably accurate date of creation; and we can make educated guesses for some about the areas of the country where they might have been made. But the nature of quilts and the particular history of quilt making, at least at this point in the development of its scholarship, deny us significant historical access beyond that.

Among the many styles and forms of American quilts there are, however, a very few that are instantly recognizable as the work of a discrete group. While we may not know their individual makers, their origins are instantly apparent. Foremost among these, most distinctive of all, are the quilts of the Amish of Pennsylvania and the Midwest. The reasons for this, and the significance of their distinctive aesthetics, are my subjects here.

Donald Kraybill and Patricia Herr have in their respective articles in this volume thoroughly and ably presented overviews of Amish history in general and quilt making in particular. My intention in this article is not simply to describe the aesthetic of Amish quilts and analyze its roots, but to discover, if possible, what particular meaning the aesthetic might have in Amish culture: Are these just beautiful geometric forms and colors of great appeal to modern eyes? Are their quilts, in this aspect, like other "folk" or "primitive" art, which sophisticated observers, outside the culture of the makers, find invigorating, satisfying, and revitalizing? Or can we also legitimately find in them a

OPPOSITE: Detail of CAT. 32.

symbolic content that expresses deeper and more specific reflections of the Amish spirit? And what of the creators? What aesthetic choices were available to women in a highly conservative society when they designed and made these extraordinary quilts? I believe one problem in studying classic Amish quilts has been that we have tended to see and examine them as exotic artifacts of an exotic culture rather than a part of the mainstream of American quilt making, as if they were a branch of the art that arose Neanderthal-like, flourished, declined, and disappeared, leaving lovely remains. I am interested in seeing where in fact they comfortably swim in the American mainstream, noting not only what makes them different from, but also what makes them part of, this school. To facilitate these inquiries I will start by setting out, in an order congenial to my discussion, those aspects of Amish, American, and quilt history that bear significantly on Amish aesthetic practices.

Originating as a separatist movement in Switzerland in the sixteenth century, the Amish, never large in numbers, were a radical offshoot of the Anabaptist movement. From the beginning they were ultraconservative, uncompromisingly independent, and certain in their faith. Rejecting, among other practices, infant baptism, and highly critical of the "professional" church hierarchies both Catholic and Protestant, they strove for a more direct relationship with God, maintaining the literal truth of His word as revealed in the Bible. The Word, they held, had an authority beyond civil dictates; they refused oaths and military service. As John Hostetler (1974, 25) wrote in his classic *Amish Society*:

> [The Anabaptists] wanted simply to have freedom of religion and a voluntary church. By their open debates with both Catholic theologians and Protestant Reformers, and by their submissive and simple obedience to the Bible, it was clear that they wished to return to a primitive, early type of Christianity. Although the wrath of the Catholic church, the Reformers, and the state was against them, in the end they won for much of the modern world the separation of church and state and freedom of religion.

Excoriated for their opposition to many traditional church practices and theological positions, they were actively persecuted for the challenge their peaceful opposition posed to ecclesiastic and civil authority. Oppressed in Switzerland, they moved on to other persecutions in other European countries, and eventually some began an exodus to the New World. Their tribulations were preserved in *Martyrs Mirror*, a record of their suffering published in the seventeenth century and still read and known by Amish. It is a constant reminder of their uniqueness; and, in fact, they think of themselves as a "chosen people" in the Biblical sense (ibid., 49).[1]

Ultimately, it was only in the Americas that the Amish sect survived; it has disappeared from the continent of its birth. It was also in the New World that their culture took on the particular stamp we associate with Old Order Amish, those of the Pennsylvania travel brochures: "The Old Order movement arose in nineteenth-century North America when both Amish and Mennonite communities were threatened with partial assimilation into the more general North American way of life. In response to this threat, conservative Amish and Mennonites organized separate church-communities to preserve what they considered the Christian way of life" (Hostetler 1989, 286).

Basic to the Amish belief system is *Gelassenheit*, obedience to God's word. The spirit of Gelassenheit expresses itself in obedience, humility, and simplicity. To Amish thinking, obedience to the will of God is the cardinal religious value. If submission is the core of Amish inner belief, separation from the world is its outer expression. "To the Amish there is a divine spiritual reality, the Kingdom of God, and a Satanic kingdom that dominates the present world. It is the duty of a Christian to keep himself 'unspotted from the world' and separate from the desires, intent and goals of the worldly person" (Hostetler 1974, 48).

The Amish signal this separateness through external signs that Kraybill (in this volume) calls "badges of identity" and "symbols of separation." A number of these signs make the Amish as distinctive as their quilts: the bearded (but not mustachioed) men in dark pants, vests, and broad-brimmed hats; the women in caps and their distinctive plain dresses, aprons, capes, and shawls; the buggies. Their clothes, grooming, and conveyances are identifying marks instantly recognizable to a broad spectrum of Americans and foreigners. Equally noticeable are the things the Amish do not use: electricity in their homes, tractors in their fields (thus their picturesque retention, of great value to the tourist industry, of horse- and mule-drawn farm equipment), cars, televisions, buttons. The use of anachronistic accoutrements is a self-fulfilling mechanism, signaling the presence of nonconformists to the world, which reacts by recognizing the nonconformists' differences, thus reinforcing the nonconformists' notion that they are different. *Gemeinschaft*, "where a common will becomes reality," describes the Amish community, much different from our sense of the same word (ibid., 101). Amish life is centered in the community rather than the individual. At the core of the Amish community is a "shared vision of life…. Members of the church willingly separate themselves from the influences of the outside society, but within the community of believers there are no separations. Family and friendship, daily life, spiritual life, and religious practice are tightly interwoven" (Granick 1990, 17).

Social control, the maintenance of orthodoxy among the Amish, is accomplished through several mechanisms and affects Amish quilt aesthetics. One of the most potent devices is community observation and judgment of its members' behavior. This is facilitated by the small size of Amish communities, church districts limited in extent by the Amish custom of holding religious services in members' homes, and the constraints of horse and buggy travel. Self-policing establishes and maintains community standards. A woman who sells fabrics to many Amish communities noted that "they can't stand to see people wearing the 'wrong' colors or fabrics" (Granick 1989, 74). Such judgments can be extremely powerful in communities such as the Amish which honor humility and conformity rather than individual accomplishment. Uncodified differences among groups, hardly noticeable to the outsider, are very significant to the Amish. "In Mifflin County, brown is a popular and widely used color among the Nebraska Amish. In New Wilmington, though its use is

39. Center Square

Last quarter nineteenth century
Amish, Lancaster County, Pennsylvania

Wool, 208.3 x 190.5 cm

Some of the material in this early example of the design is a wool-silk combination.

Collection of the author

certainly permitted, most women consider it too ugly for a dress" (ibid.). (It is thus too ugly also for a quilt.) "The members of each community practice nearly complete conformity in terms of clothing style and color. They purchase the same fabrics and sew their clothing in the manner agreed upon by the group" (ibid.). Clearly, this affects the aesthetics of their quilts.

Another mechanism is reverence for the past. The Amish value their forebears' ways of doing things. Nothing is changed just for the sake of change; it is a means of fostering necessary stability. This, too, affects how their quilts are made and how they look. Specific rules for living are codified in the *Ordnung*; each Amish group develops its own, and they vary widely from group to group. Though usually unwritten, they are quite specific, and are known to and understood by all members, who have assented to them. They bear considerably on our consideration of Amish creative attitudes. Hostetler (1974, 59-60) quotes the Ordnung for an Amish congregation in Pike County, Ohio in 1950, which is worth repeating at some length.

> Since it is the duty of the church, especially in this day and age, to decide what is fitting and proper and also what is not fitting and proper for a Christian to do (in points that are not clearly stated in the Bible), we have considered it needful to publish this booklet listing some rules and ordinances of a Christian Church.
>
> No ornamental bright, showy form-fitting immodest or silk-like clothing of any kind. Colors such as bright red, orange, yellow and pink are not allowed. Amish form of clothing to be followed as a general rule. Costly Sunday clothing to be discouraged. Dresses not shorter than half-way [*sic*] between knees and floor, nor over eight inches from floor. Longer advisable. Clothing in every way modest, serviceable and as simple as scripturally possible. Only outside pockets allowed are one on work eberhem or vomas and pockets on large overcoats. Dress shoes, if any, to be plain and black only. No high heels and pomp slippers, dress socks, if any, to be black except white for foot hygiene for both sexes. A plain, unshowy suspender without buckles.
>
> Hat to be black with no less than 3-inch rim and not extremely high in crown. No stylish impression in any hat. No pressed trousers. No sweaters.
>
> Women to wear shawls, bonnets, and capes in public. Aprons to be worn at all times. No adorning of hair among either sex such as parting of hair among men and curling or waving among women.
>
> No decorations of any kind in buildings inside or out. No fancy yard fences. Linoleum, oilcloth, shelf and wall paper [*sic*] to be plain and unshowy. Over-stuffed furniture or any luxury items forbidden. No doilies or napkins. No large mirrors, (fancy glassware), statues or wall pictures for decorations.
>
> [No embroidery work of any kind.] No boughten [*sic*] dolls. Weddings should be simple and without decorations. No airfilled rubber tires. Musical instruments or different voices singing not permissible. No insurance. No photographs.

While such rules might seem rigid when set to paper, they are in normal practice an oral, commonly understood tradition, subject to continual change and modification; it is, in effect, the community's means of dealing with necessary accommodation, their interface with the larger culture that surrounds them. The Ordnung is a sophisticated device that provides both a guideline for group behavior and a mechanism for its change. Such voluntarily accepted rules or understandings significantly affected the aesthetics of Amish quilts directly, where, for instance, there were restrictions on using certain colors, or where, as in several conservative districts, the bishops forbade piecing itself as too worldly, so all quilts were of whole cloth. Successful and pleasing virtuosity or innovation could attract unwanted attention and criticism; one might go to the edge of, but not beyond, certain boundaries. Pride is the enemy—in personal accomplishment, ownership, display, and drawing attention to oneself.

These social mechanisms made Amish quilt makers keenly aware of the limits of community tolerance for innovation and the depth of community approval and support for tradition. Thus they were encouraged to create within relatively fixed boundaries, innovating with circumspection, and these constraints were instrumental in forming their aesthetic.

I have emphasized thus far the obligatory aspects of Amish life, means developed to promote conformity and comfort within its bounds. Conformity and its taskmaster obedience are basic to Amish life. But it needs to be emphasized equally that the Amish do not comprise a monolithic culture; different groups within it and individuals within the groups exhibit wide variances in attitude and practice beyond their core beliefs. A casual onlooker, observing the Amish in the many places in the United States they now live, might initially note a remarkable homogeneity of appearance and behavior from one group to the next. In clothes and conveyances, and, more subtly, in work practices, social interchanges and other manifestations of culture, there are marked similarities. A student of Amish culture observing the same people, however, would see something quite different. He or she would discern the subtle differences in clothing, hat styles, buggy colors, work practices, tools, and a myriad of other details that distinguish different Amish groups and were born of differences in attitude and interpretation of beliefs. And if this person were persistent enough to know some Amish well, he or she would discover a diversity of personalities, predilections, and interests. It is important to an understanding of Amish quilts to recognize that both the press of conformity and the urgings of individuality are encompassed within the structure of Amish society.

Given their basic beliefs, what sort of society did the Amish form and maintain in this country? The New World offered them two essential things: freedom from persecution and cheap land. While rising land prices have forced some Amish to take up other occupations, during the period of quilt making of interest to us here, the Amish were largely farmers. Walter Kolmorgen (1942), looking at the Lancaster County Amish in a government study of rural life in the 1940s, said, "The Amish farmer is wedded to the land not only by a deep and long tradition of good agricultural practices, but farming has also become one of the tenets of the Amish religion. A rural way of life is essential to these people so that their nonconformist practices may be perpetuated."

In a manner difficult for most of us to grasp, Amish culture centers on religion; duty to God comes first. Hostetler (1974, 10) notes, "Amish life is distinctive in that it is pervasively religious. The core values of the community are religious beliefs." This affects attitudes towards status, as Kraybill notes (in this volume): "The conventional marks of social status—education, income, occupation and consumer goods—are largely missing from Amish society. Their agrarian heritage placed most members on common social footing." (This does not mean, of course, that there is no status recognition in Amish communities; it relates, however, to Amish values, rather than those of the surrounding culture.)

"The Amish community," says Hostetler (ibid., 101), "is a ceremonial community…. Intensive participation provides the individual with a sense of order and destiny." They prefer the old to the new, and in that sense are a change-rejective culture, in sharp contrast to the industrialized, change-acceptant culture that surrounds them. Kraybill writes (in this volume): "Amish society pivots on a delicate tension between tradition and social change. In a consumer world where new is considered better, the Amish tilt toward the past." Not all things are rejected; they are particularly concerned

40. Framed Center

Beginning of the nineteenth century
Non-Amish, Pennsylvania

Glazed calamanca (wool), 243.8 x 223.5 cm

This sort of glazed wool quilt was possibly the model for the first pieced Lancaster Amish quilts in the Framed Center style.

America Hurrah, NYC

about those which, as Kraybill notes, "might undermine community life" (ibid.). Each church district makes its own decision about innovations. Some use telephones in shops and businesses, others do not. "Modern bathrooms, the latest gas appliances, and air powered tools are common in some Amish settlements. Families in the more conservative communities still use outhouses and do not have refrigerators" (ibid.). While there clearly is no general rule that may be applied to all Amish groups, the basic attitude seems to be that things which better life without threatening core values may be assimilated.

The Amish view of nature is influenced by their religious attitude: "The Amish do not seek to master nature or to work against the elements, but to work with them. The affinity between Amish society and nature in the form of lands, terrains, and vegetation is expressed in various degrees of intensity" (Hostetler 1974, 10). Man's goal is not to master His nature, but to master his nature. He serves God by bending his will to Him.

Amish society is pervasively, but not monolithically, patriarchal. Men are leaders in each church district. Women can vote in church meetings and nominate men for ecclesiastical positions, but are excluded from leadership roles. Attitudes towards women are biblically sanctioned. "With regard to the woman's role in religious services the teaching of the Apostle Paul is literally obeyed: 'Let the woman learn in silence with all subjection'" (ibid., 151). In leadership activities, the woman is not "to usurp authority over the man." In the province of the family, equality is more apparent. Patricia Herr (in this volume) notes, "Women always have had a position of importance within Amish society." The good housewife is essential in a farming family with numerous children; and there are many avenues to status. Hostetler (1974, 19) notes, "Within her role as homemaker she has greater possibility of achieving status recognition than the suburban housewife." In the family economic unit, the husband's provinces are the fields, the work animals, the barns, and equipment; his wife's are the kitchen garden, the chickens, the house, the children. But the boundaries are not rigid; Kraybill (in this volume) notes that both husband and wife may ask each other for help in their separate spheres: "Although husband and wife preside over distinct spheres of domestic life, many tasks are shared. A wife may ask her husband to assist in the garden and he may ask her to help in the barn, field, or shop.... In the words of one Amish man, 'The wife is not a servant; she is the queen and the husband is the king.'"

Hostetler (1974, 151-52) notes the constrained emotion in Amish life: "Personal relationships between husband and wife are quiet and sober, with no apparent demonstration of affection. The relationship is strikingly different from the way sentiments are indicated and affection expressed in American society. Patterns of conversation vary among Amish mates, but terms of endearment, or gestures which would indicate any overt expression of affection, are conspicuously absent.... The bond between husband and wife tends to be one of respect rather than personal attraction based on romantic love."

Farming is a labor-intensive occupation, and it requires great human effort to run a successful farm without the benefit of engine-powered, labor-saving equipment. Moreover, the Amish definition of self-sufficiency includes taking care of their elderly within the family; this and other societal goals require extended families with many members. Thus the Amish tend to have large families, a 1967 study finding an average of seven to nine children in each (ibid., 82). "The maintenance of their particular way of life makes them conscious of fertility, in their fields, their kitchen gardens, their families. The birth of a child brings joy to the family and community, for there will be another dish washer or wood chopper, and another church member" (ibid., 153).

Let us turn now to their quilts. The first significant body of Amish settlers arrived in the New World during the third through sixth decades of the eighteenth century, and settled in Pennsylvania. Little is known with certainty about their bed furnishings. It can be assumed, however, that they had been familiar with in the Old World, and used in the New, what are called "featherbeds," essentially sacks stuffed with feathers and used as both mattress and cover; their neighbors in Pennsylvania used such bed furnishings. (Elkanah Watson, a New Englander who stayed in a Reamstown, Pennsylvania inn in 1777, recorded in his journal, "I was placed between two beds, without sheets or pillows. This, I was told, was the prevailing custom, but which, as far as my experience goes, adds little to promote the sleep or comfort of a stranger" [Lichten 1946, 168].)

Benjamin Rush (1745-1813), writing on early Pennsylvania life, had this to say: "The German farmers live frugally in their families in respect to diet, furniture and apparel. The furniture in their house is plain and useful...they cover themselves in winter with light featherbeds instead of blankets" (Granick 1989, 23). It is likely that blankets and coverlets were also in use among German settlers in Pennsylvania. Herr (in this volume) illustrates the earliest documented Amish bedcovering, a woven coverlet dated 1836, and notes: "The primary bed covering used by the Pennsylvania

41. Framed Center

End of the eighteenth century
Non-Amish, Northeastern United States

Cotton, 241.3 x 191.8 cm

A two-material quilt of a type which likely influenced the earliest Amish pieced quilt designs.

Collection of the New York State Historical Association, Cooperstown, New York, F-260.48

German colonist was the handwoven coverlet, which would have lain over the plaid linen tick cover that surrounded the feather tick." She mentions also the existence of Amish professional weavers in the eighteenth and nineteenth centuries.

It is not clear when the first quilts were made by any quilt makers in America, but it is certain they were not in general use during the Colonial period. Quilts were, at that time, a luxury, and those which appear in American inventories were very likely imported; they were advertised in the eighteenth century by importers in the major Eastern coastal cities. Whole cloth quilts from India, Persia, and China had been imported to Europe before the Amish hegira, and whole cloth quilts of silk and linen, likely emulating some of the imports, were made in England and other countries in the seventeenth century. But both imports and homemades were clearly luxury goods for the upper classes, perhaps known to, but not likely used by, the Amish.

It is my feeling now that patchwork quilts were an English invention of the late seventeenth or early eighteenth century. While there do exist (but not in the U.S.) several pieced quilts with fairly convincing histories from the early 1700s, it is generally thought that Americans began making quilts in any number later in that century. So during the first period of Amish settlement, they did not use quilts as bed covers. In that, their practice was in concert with most of their neighbors.

Some Amish who had originally settled in Pennsylvania migrated west, like other Americans, first within Pennsylvania, then farther into the Midwest. They formed their first settlement in Holmes County, Ohio in 1807 and went on to other areas (Hostetler 1974, 74). Early in the nineteenth century other Amish groups went directly from Europe to the Midwest, the emotional way there having been prepared by their compatriots who had settled earlier in the New World; between 1815 and 1840, for instance, Amish from Bavaria and Alsatia settled in Indiana, Ohio, and Ontario, Canada (ibid., 40). So by the first decades of the nineteenth century there were significant Amish presences in a number of American states and Canada.

In Pennsylvania, Ohio, and Indiana, the Amish settled near other Americans who made quilts. Between the time of the first Amish settlement in Pennsylvania and the first beyond, quilt making in America had begun and experienced considerable stylistic development. In 1810 a young woman from New England stayed in a Berks County, Pennsylvania inn and noted, "Our bed to sleep on was straw and then a feather bed for covering—The pillows contain'd nearly a single handful of feathers, & were cover'd with most curious and dirty patchwork, I ever saw—We had one bed quilt and one sheet…" (Lichten 1946, 169). (Perhaps this was an improvement on the 1777 accommodations noted previously.)

By the time of extensive Amish settlement in the Midwest in the mid-nineteenth century, quilt design had begun to mature and distinctly American styles were developing. The Amish, though exposed to quilts for almost a century by that time, were apparently still not making quilts. Perhaps the most important reason for this was their innate resistance to taking up a pursuit foreign to their craft traditions, one so identified with their "English" neighbors, and one in which they might have seen considerable potential for self-aggrandizement and the development of pride. Their participation, in my opinion, had to await the outcome of a social change which had had a significant effect on American quilt making, the birth and development of the "cult of domesticity" or, as Gerda Lerner (1979, 190) described it, the "cult of true womanhood."

America toward the mid-nineteenth century was still largely rural; Larkin notes, "as late as 1840, no more than one in nine were urban even in this modest sense [of living in communities]" (1988, 6). The American Revolution and the revolution of industrialization disrupted many of the ancient economic and social patterns that had characterized American life since the earliest days of settlement. Expectations were greatly altered, and alternatives to the age-old, family-based system of rural and urban undertakings developed. People could sell their labor to entrepreneurs, moving from the country to establish themselves in the new centers of manufacturing. Characteristic ancient divisions of labor among men, women, and children were irrevocably altered (Hymowitz and Weissman 1981, 64-66):

> Following the Revolutionary War and in the first decades of the 1800s a new middle class emerged in the Northeast. While the majority of Americans continued to live on farms, members of this middle class lived in towns and cities and derived their wealth from commerce.... The business of business took middle class men away from their homes, leaving women alone in them. Women of the middle class were isolated from the world of men and commerce.... On colonial farms, where the labor of both sexes was equally necessary, men and women were partners.... [This, of course, is the pattern Amish society has continued to follow.]
>
> Among the new middle class, home and family came to be seen as separate from the world of work and money.... In their homes, middle-class women continued to perform their traditional work.... What they did, however, was no longer considered "real work" because, unlike men, they earned no money thereby. For the first time in America a class of women emerged who were seen as being "supported" by their husbands. No longer partners, they had become dependents.... In the 1700s it was possible to think of a woman as strong, brave, daring, hardy, adventurous. By the 1800s these qualities were thought to apply only to men.

What was the result of this? Middle-class women were increasingly cut off from significant economic opportunities. The social and economic gap widened between them and their sisters working in mills and factories. "Many of the trades women had practiced in colonial times now required formal training, from which women were excluded" (ibid., 65). This led to a new emotional centering on the home. Conceptualizations about home and "the women and children who resided there, safe from the 'cruelties of the marketplace,' came to assume new levels of emotional importance" (ibid.).

Men were seen as economic warriors, plunging valiantly into the tumult and dangers of the world to bring home sustenance to their families; women were to be the carriers of culture; it was their duty to preserve the "finer things" and inculcate children with Christian virtues. With this went an emphasis on women's "sensitive" and artistic natures. Widely-read ladies' periodicals catered to this new image, suggesting appropriate dress, deportment, and child-rearing practices. Refinement was a goal; coarseness was to be excluded from family life. Clothing styles changed to accommodate the new social rigidity and prudishness. Where women had in the preceding Empire period worn light, simple, form-fitting, and revealing gowns based on classical models, they now were increasingly encased in layers of clothing and undergarments that masked their forms and impeded free movement.

With this new burdening of the body and mind came notions of proper feminine leisure-time pursuits. Chief among these was needlework. Throughout America's previous history, most women had sewn or worked textiles. Much of this work was done of necessity: growing and harvesting the raw materials for, and making, textiles; sewing and knitting clothing; producing bed covers of different types from homewoven coverlets (though most were probably done by professional weavers) to rough quilts. Some were made for pleasure or prestige: embroidered bed furnishings, samplers and needlework pictures, fancy quilts, stenciled spreads, and white work. But women of all classes sewed. In the domestic cult, it was the status aspect of sewing that was emphasized; sewing was seen as a genteel occupation, an outward sign of feminine virtue, and the ladies' magazines made a continual offering of "refined" make-work projects to use up newly gained leisure time.

It is clear that quilt production was given great impetus by this movement, manifesting itself during the early period in such productions as the elaborate Baltimore Album quilts and, at the end, in silk and velvet Crazy quilts, which were barely functional and certainly not practical. (But then, in terms of actual use, neither was the Baltimore Album quilt; both types were made for show.) Needlework became a national craze, and quilt making was a major expression of the urge. While many busywork sewing projects which were a product of the cult of domesticity were discarded as America met the twentieth century, quilt making had, in my opinion, become and continued as a cult it its own right.

42. Framed Center or Center Medallion

End of the eighteenth century
Non-Amish, Virginia

Cotton, 255.9 x 254.0 cm

A high-style quilt with pieced elements typical of those made in England and America in the eighteenth century; these quilts were a basic design source for Lancaster Amish Center Square and Diamond quilts.

Collection of the Mount Vernon Ladies' Association

Three advances, two technological and one stylistic, vastly increased the output of quilts in America in the latter half of the nineteenth century; the three had the combined effect of making quilts cheaper and easier to make, so that more Americans were able to afford the raw materials and had the skills to pursue the craft. The stylistic advance was the elaboration of the block style. In the earliest extant English and American quilts, dating to the eighteenth century, almost all in the Framed Center format, blocks in simple patterns (Four Patch, Nine Patch, Variable Star) are found as border elements in pieced or pieced-and-appliquéd examples; in some cases they comprise the entire quilt. Most quilts in the central medallion style were constructed from the middle out, so one was dealing with an ever-growing textile. Such high-style quilts in pieced, appliqué, or combinations of pieced-and-appliquéd work, and whole cloth quilts, required relatively large, clean areas in which they could be worked, and few Americans in the early nineteenth century lived in such surroundings. American quilt makers, however, recognized the efficiency of the block as a work method, understanding that such squares were the easiest in which to develop complex designs. The blocks could be lap-worked, obviating the need for a large work area except at the end, when the quilt was assembled and quilted. (Also, as the century progressed, more Americans lived in larger houses and had more leisure time and fewer sewing skills. Thus, they had more space to work on quilts, as well as the time to do so, and found block-style work easy to do.)

Another advantage of the style was that a relatively unskilled seamstress could assemble individual blocks, then the blocks into a top; they did not require the high degree of sewing skills which were necessary to produce the great high style quilts of the early nineteenth century, yet powerful, complex, and pleasing designs could be easily produced using the method.

The block style had been developing slowly since the eighteenth century. After the first quarter of the nineteenth century, we see the block style becoming the predominant overall style in American quilts, establishing pieced quilts as the major type made. As time went on there was much visual experimentation with sashes, block orientation, more open space (pieced blocks alternating with solid color or white blocks), and the creation of blocks which linked to other blocks to form primary overall designs, etc. This work method and style was well established by the time of the arrival of new technology which affected quilt making. One might logically assume that as long as quilt makers had available only relatively expensive "natural" (derived from vegetation and minerals) dyed cottons, few quilts would be made, and those largely by the well-to-do; and in fact, until the latter half of the nineteenth century, that appears to be the pattern. There are comparatively few pre-1850 quilts, and most of those appear to me to have been made in families of relative means. Aniline or

43. Center Square

ca. 1900

Amish, Lancaster County, Pennsylvania

Wool, 185.4 x 188.0 cm

Note the similarities in format to the Center Medallion quilt, FIG. 42.

Collection of the author

"synthetic" dyes derived from coal tars were developed shortly after the mid-nineteenth century in Germany. Within a decade they were being used in fabric dyeing, and quickly replaced, with a wide range of brilliant hues, the more expensive and more tonally limited, natural dyes. These synthetic dyes, along with improved cotton textile manufacturing techniques, brought, by mid-century, a body of cheaper, bright cotton textiles ever increasing thereafter in palette and print choice.

The second technological innovation was the sewing machine, which was being aggressively and successfully mass-marketed by the 1860s. By 1855, *Godey's Lady's Book*, the periodical of the domestic cult, was saying: "These valuable aids to female industry are becoming quite a familiar thing in private families"; in 1860, the periodical stated: "In quilting, and all kinds of stitching, they seem indispensable...." Kouwenhoven (1948, 42) notes, "In one year of the 1870s, 600,000 sewing machines were sold."

The result of the greater availability and affordability of material, the new ease of sewing by machine, the large pool of American women trained in sewing skills, and the interest in needlework generated by the cult of domesticity was an explosion in quilt making and design innovation, and a quilt cult.

It was also during this period that the "Scrap Bag Myth" was born. This myth, a chapter within the larger myth of a pre-industrial American Golden Age, postulates self-reliant ancestors of unimpeachable integrity, stoicism in the face of privation and danger, wisdom, and, perhaps above all, thrift. It was likely a conservative reaction to growing middle-class prosperity and social changes and the fears, which often accompany such upheavals, of a deterioration of national character. These paragons can be seen in the archetypical Yankee, the Frontiersman, the Woodsman, the Mountain Man, and other characters who populate our national body of legend. Their character traits were equally ascribed to the women who had shared the American experience with them, and to them were additionally given the qualities of Penelope: virtue, fortitude, and skills at household management in which, in the American version, thrift was given preeminent seating. (It should be noted that the very qualities of independence praised in these women by their ostensible descendents were in fact despised by the Victorian middle class; in the family informed by the cult of domesticity, such self-reliant women would have had scant place.)

Quilts had a significant place in this myth. Even as a cult of quilt making developed in the 1870s and 1880s, the myth-making was underway. In popular literature, in paintings and prints, quilt makers were depicted as exemplars of idealized feminine roles, and their quilts as the quintessential American products, silk purses from sow's ears, things of great practical value and beauty made by applying intelligence and virtuous industry to otherwise useless raw materials, the leftover cloth in the scrap bag.

The Westward Movement refined and enlarged the myth: the pioneer woman, faced with the rigors, dangers, and deprivations of the wilderness, and needing warm bed covers for the survival of her family, created from scraps of worn-out clothing and bits of otherwise useless cloth the quilts that were her family's salvation and her creative glory.

As is true of all myths, this myth was not made completely from whole cloth; its structure was supported by scraps of stitched-in truth. America's pre-industrial economy was one of scarcity for most; and just as many Americans now living have attitudes towards work and money formed during the Depression more than a half century ago. In early industrial America the majority of our population remembered childhoods if not of want, then certainly where care and thrift were required to survive. The common memory was not of abundance, but of making do. As this history became part of the American legend, quilts became part of its nostalgia. It is a tribute to quilts' potency in our culture that they assumed such a prominent role in the drama.

Unquestionably, there were places where quilts were made of necessity, where there was no money to buy blankets and no ability to weave them, and where household economy dictated making warm covers rather than purchasing them; I have seen such quilts, and I have examined some of their verifiable histories. I believe, however, that this type of quilt production was a phenomenon largely of the later nineteenth century. I also believe the more common situation was one of a two-track system in which the same women made both utilitarian and "better" quilts. The latter might in fact be divided again, into those quilts with carefully-made tops and good quilting which were nevertheless made for ordinary family use (many of this type show signs of hard use, the fulfillment of their function), and "show" quilts, often with floral appliqué, broderie perse, or other high-style decorative techniques. The last were normally used sparingly, and sometimes not at all. But from their beginnings as high-style, prestige textiles in the eighteenth century through the development of many new styles in the nineteenth, to the twentieth-century revival and "art" quilts, the vast majority of American quilts—whole-cloth, pieced, and appliquéd—were as much designed works as bed covers. Even common utility quilts usually show careful organization of the parts of their tops for a pleasing visual effect. There is no question in my mind that quilt making has always been, first and foremost, an aesthetic medium.

While this is not the place to parse this truth to the end, it is evident if one studies the aesthetics and history of quilts and disregards the myths. Perhaps the most significant piece of evidence for me is this: Of the tens of thousands of pieced quilts I have examined, the vast majority have backs of whole cloth, new at the time the quilts were made. This indicates that material was purchased to make the backs, which normally would not have been seen; if quilts were truly objects in whose formation thrift and utility were the primary motives, the backs would logically have been pieced from scraps left over from home clothes production; and, if the romantic histories were true, of pieces salvaged from worn-out garments. Trust me: There is hardly a quilt maker who ever pieced any part of a quilt from sections of worn-out garments. The finished textiles would not have survived enough washings to justify either the savings on textile costs or the labor involved.

Additionally, when one can examine unwashed pieced cotton quilts, it soon becomes evident that many or most use materials purchased to be cut up and formed into patterns. So both the back and tops of pieced quilts support this: Quilt making was, and even more is now, an aesthetic medium.

44. Diamond in a Square

Maker unknown, 1930-1940
Amish, Lancaster County, Pennsylvania

Wool and cotton, 203.2 x 205.1 cm
Quilting patterns: roses, rose wreaths, scallops

The artist initialed the quilt "LB" in embroidery in a corner of the binding.

Tietze & Hodosh Collection

The cult of the quilt continued into the twentieth century, receiving impetus through a revival of interest in needlework during the Colonial Revival period (late nineteenth to early twentieth century). During that period, interest in the artifacts of an earlier American life, disdained as old fashioned by the Victorians, was born. Early quilts were among the objects collected and studied; with this went a great deal of romanticizing about Colonial life, and many of the fictions about quilts originated or perpetuated then are with us still. Certainly there may be seen in the period another search for identity and values in a society undergoing rapid change.

Other mini-revivals took place as the century progressed. So many quilts were made during this long period by people for whom they offered insignificant utilitarian value, that there should be little doubt of their mythic dimension. Nor has that ended. The revivals of interest that have taken place over the past several decades have given quilts a status they never before enjoyed, and the interest is worldwide. I would think there are now more women making quilts than ever before in the craft's history, at a time when they are absolutely unnecessary as instruments of survival for their makers. (Another result of our modern interest in the form: Amish quilts are known and revered around the world for their aesthetic merit.)

45. Framed Center Strip quilt made largely of floral strip-style chintzes

ca. 1835
Non-Amish, Pennsylvania

Chintzes (cotton), 254.0 x 243.8 cm

This style of early quilt was most likely the source for the Amish Bars design. Note the inner border with its small corner blocks, a design characteristic of many Lancaster Amish quilts.

America Hurrah, NYC

Let us now consider where Amish quilts are to be found in this history, how their particular aesthetic was formed, and how we are to interpret it.

Though I will be concentrating in the beginning on the quilts of the Amish of the Lancaster County, Pennsylvania area, many of my general observations would apply equally to the quilts of the Amish of other areas (primarily the Midwest). Though quilts appear in Amish inventories in the 1830s, the earliest surviving dated Amish quilt yet found has embroidered on it the initials "BP" and the date "1849." It is of indigo-blue cotton on each side, bound in a contrasting edging (a trait which was to continue in Pennsylvania Amish quilts), its predominant design in its quilting patterns. Another similar quilt dated 1869, twenty years later, found among the Amish in Indiana but thought to have originated in Lancaster County, Pennsylvania, is of blue glazed cotton on one side and brown wool on the other. Its quilting patterns are similar to the 1849 quilt, with a wide border defined by interlocking curved parallel lines framing a central field, which in the earlier quilt has a fairly elaborate ensemble of patterns and in the latter is a simple grid.

What do these quilts tell us? First, they indicate an almost certain borrowing from neighbors of a style anachronistic at the time of its adoption. They strongly resemble the calamanco (glazed wool) whole cloth quilts (sometimes erroneously called "linsey-woolsey" quilts), heavy covers often made with an indigo glazed wool top and a brown wool back. These are found predominantly in the northeast and have normally been attributed to American quilt makers. While some may have been made here, I think many may have been imported; no evidence of their domestic manufacture has yet appeared, and I believe there is some reason, because of their materials, construction, stuffing material and style of quilting, and the fact that many are found in Canada, to attribute them to professional male English quilt makers who produced them for home use and export. Nevertheless, they were in wide use in this country; many have been found in Pennsylvania, and they were a possible model for these early Amish quilts.

There are other possibilities, however. Herr (in this volume) has pointed out that these early Amish quilts also resemble "whole cloth silk and wool Quaker quilts from neighboring Chester and Philadelphia counties." One piece of evidence that points to Quaker quilts as the original inspiration for the Amish is the sparse stuffing of these early pieces. The calamanco quilts are normally thickly stuffed with wool and coarsely, if sometimes interestingly, quilted, thick quilts for cold climates. Quaker quilts are distinctly more elegant, and have much thinner stuffing. This, of course, makes them less efficient as covers but more likely as mediums for fine quilting. Lancaster Amish quilts from the beginning followed the latter pattern, thinly stuffed and finely quilted, and the Amish had contact with Pennsylvania Quakers. Also, some nineteenth-century Welsh quilts are remarkably similar to the fully developed Lancaster Amish designs in both overall formats and quilting patterns, and there were Welsh immigrants living in Pennsylvania. Speaking of Welsh quilts in her book, *Traditional British Quilts*, Dorothy Osler (1987, 142) says, "All types of quilts were made—whole cloth, patchwork, appliqué…. Patchwork, though bold and colorful, was often of a more utilitarian nature, with medallion quilts by far the most popular…. Medallion quilts…were produced for both 'best' and 'everyday' quilts…." (What Osler calls the "medallion" quilt is called "center medallion" in the United States and forms the design basis, I believe, of the Amish Diamond quilt.)

One quilt Osler (1987, 142) illustrates had in its quilting patterns a "cable twist outer border." She notes,

> Welsh quilts were usually wool-filled but both cotton and wool fabrics were used for the covers…but the Welsh were particularly fond of using wool fabrics…both for patchwork and whole cloth quilts. One Carmarthenshire quilter, born in 1870, recalled that cloth woven in the local mills…was popular for quilts in her youth, in two colours, such as rose or blue with maroon…. The Welsh had a fondness for strong colours—red, magenta, maroon, dark blue, green, purple, brown and even black…."

These are apt descriptions of Amish quilt color choices, emphasizing clearly an area that warrants further research.

The 1869 quilt mentioned above appears at the lower end of the time horizon for Amish quilts.

Few quilts appear in Amish inventories until the 1870s, but from then on "Amish families from all communities listed quilts among their possessions with increasing frequency" (Granick 1989, 46). Surviving examples from this decade and the next, however, are extraordinarily rare; there are very few even from the 1890s. However, it is clear that a more general Amish involvement in quilt making began in those decades, and this is significant as it coincides with the maturing design tradition and great surge of quilt making in America. It is, in my opinion, likely that the Amish were at least partly beguiled by the ferment of quilt making and quilt mythmaking happening around them. The technical features and social history of fine Lancaster Amish quilts, their "show" quilts, indicate that the craft was for them, as for other Americans, an aesthetic medium. Additionally, I think it likely that the Amish, long after its inception, were directly or indirectly influenced by the cult of domesticity. Certainly, they adopted some of its baggage. One can see it in their use of the Crazy quilt format, and the rare twentieth-century Amish quilts that incorporated surface embellishment of fancy stitch embroidery, particularly the "turkey track" pattern. Sometimes they put it on their Crazy quilts, sometimes they used it on other styles. Though not common, the adoption of such totally superfluous embroidery, a use of time and material to create something with no functional value, indicates the Amish were not entirely immune to the temptations of high style. There were also a very few quilts with appliqué; this last type had come to be seen as "best" quilts in "English" society, because they mimicked high style floral-designed textiles, and were extravagant of materials: the designs, cut from whole cloth, were applied to a whole cloth top.

Though no social phenomenon could have been more inimical to their basic attitudes than the domestic cult, the sewing and quilt making phenomenon it encouraged was not out of keeping with Amish interests. Amish women, long after most other Americans had stopped, were still making clothes for their families, so there was among them a reservoir of sewing skills and a continuing interest in needlework. They had early adopted the treadle sewing machine, a labor-saving device that evidently did not threaten basic Amish interests; they use it still. They were surrounded by and no doubt interacted with neighbors who had a keen interest in quilt making. (Pennsylvania was one of the most active quilt making areas in America.) And in a culture in which men were the titular or symbolic heads of almost all enterprises, we must recognize the appeal to Amish women of a female-oriented activity which embodied cultural values of interest to them, and from which men were largely excluded. It was perhaps inevitable that creative Amish women would find a reason to make quilts.

While there may have been other factors prompting the Amish to make quilts, they were perhaps little different from those that urged other Americans to the same endeavor. It is ironic that the preoccupations of a burgeoning bourgeois society, whose values diverged so sharply from those of the Amish, were most likely at least in part responsible for the beginnings of Amish quilt making. Because we see the first manifestations of distinctly Amish design in quilts during the three decades at the end of the nineteenth century, we should consider 1870 the beginning of the classic period of Amish quilts, one which went until the 1940s in Lancaster County and several decades later in the Midwest.

The development of Lancaster County Amish quilt design proceeded logically from those early whole-cloth examples. It is generally felt that the next design to appear was what collectors and writers have called the Center Square; see Figure 21 in Herr's article, showing a quilt dated 1875 on the fabric, the earliest dated example yet found of this design, from the collection of Patricia Herr and her husband Donald. Its derivation has discernible antecedents. If you look at the 1869 whole cloth quilt discussed previously (Figure 20 in Herr's article), you can see that it has a wide outer border delineated by cable quilting, and an inner design field filled with grid quilting. It is not a long stretch to think of making that simple format from two different materials of contrasting colors to create the Center Square quilt (FIG. 39); the contrasting edging, characteristic of Lancaster County Amish quilts, is already in place at that early date. The prototype for this design exists in a number of American quilt types of the late eighteenth to early nineteenth centuries. One can see it in wool (calamanco) quilts (FIG. 40), in some late eighteenth- to early nineteenth-century American cotton quilts which used a central panel of one printed linen or cotton framed by a wide border of another print (see the example in Figure 41, which also has corner blocks, a characteristic of many Lancaster Amish quilts), and in the fancier Center Medallion high-style quilts of the same period (see the example in Figure 42 in comparison to the Lancaster Amish Center Square quilt in Figure 43).

It is also with the early Center Square Amish quilts that we see the other most significant aesthetic development in Lancaster Amish quilts: The choice to use fine wools rather than cotton for the tops. This was innovative in American quilts, in which the general pattern was to use both coarse wools and cotton for utilitarian quilts, but cotton almost exclusively for fine quilts. There was a limited use of fine wools by non-Amish quilt makers during the nineteenth century, as in the Quaker quilts mentioned previously. In the 1870s and 1880s, a considerable number of Log Cabin quilts were made in fine wools, some in plain colors, others in patterned materials; a quantity of these have been collected in Pennsylvania, where they were no doubt made. While the Amish most likely saw such quilts (their very similar Log Cabin quilts appear a decade or more later), it is more likely that their use of wool was a conservative retention of earlier quilt models and a decision to use in their quilts the same expensive materials they used for their finer clothing. This is born out by their use of unpatterned wool cloth for the tops and, almost always, conservatively patterned cottons for the backs. It is in keeping with the normal (and logical) American pattern of using the best and more expensive materials on the side of the quilt that would be seen. The Lancaster Amish did not use patterned cloth for any of their clothing, demonstrating again that the quilt occupied a strange middle ground in Amish culture, in which some things that might not be permissible elsewhere could be tolerated there. Further, the use of fine wools gives additional proof of creative intent. The quilts were made of a material that was not easy to wash, attracted moths, and was particularly prone to show stains prominently.

Herr (in this volume) quotes a quilter in her sixties who had been raised as Amish and who reminisced thus about the 1940s and "best quilts":

> It is very fine stitching…10 stitches to the inch…and it is batiste. And of course the colors are dark, and they always chose [*sic*] dark because you would never wash it. You would just hang it up, air them out.[2]

They were clearly made as "best" quilts, to be carefully used, preserved, and (proudly?) displayed. These thinly stuffed quilts, as warming to the spirit as the body, were more the crowns than the covers of Amish beds.

The wools used in Lancaster Amish quilts were of a number of types and weaves, and had different visual effects. Wool and silk combinations are occasionally seen, usually in earlier quilts; they have an unobtrusive sheen which can bring a subtle glow to their color areas. Another wool, called "henrietta," which was used in earlier quilts, had brown warps overlaid by those wefts that gave the material its surface color; the effect is of a livelier surface with considerable depth. ("Henrietta" was also used to describe other types of wool favored by the Amish.) Fine plain-weave wools advertised as "batistes" were widely used in Lancaster County, and can sometimes be found in combination with henriettas in a quilt. Quilts made with the batistes exclusively have the flattest, most intensely colored surfaces of Lancaster quilts, and are, with henriettas, the standard materials of the classic period. Where batistes were used with brown-warped henrietta, the differences in surface quality create subtle shifts of light.

Wool crepes and part-wool fabrics appear in Amish quilts during the last several decades of the "classic" period, when some of the favored materials were no longer available. The crepes have a nubbier surface than the earlier henriettas and batistes, and create quilts with a slightly "woolier" appearance that absorbs and reflects light differently. To my eye they do not have the intense inner glow often seen in earlier wool quilts; their surfaces seem to have less depth. With the outbreak of World War II, the good quality wool textiles beloved of generations of Lancaster Amish quilt makers became difficult to obtain, and they were forced to use other materials, including rayon, in their clothes and quilt making.

Rayon had been introduced to the American public in the 1920s, and the Lancaster Amish began to use it in their quilts in small amounts before that decade ended. (Strangely, other quilt makers were less keen on it, perhaps because it was first marketed as a silk substitute, is not as easy to cut and control in sewing as cotton or wool, and does not clean as easily as cotton. In this case, the "English" were more conservative than the Amish. Perhaps because the Amish were using it as a wool substitute in a "best" quilt, they did not anticipate subjecting it to heavy use.)

Rayon has significantly different surface and reflective qualities from wool, it is visually livelier, and where it was used in an Amish quilt in combination with the latter material, it adds often vivid highlights. Sometimes, as in the Diamond quilt (FIG. 44), it is experienced as a glossier or silkier surface. Few other American quilt makers made quilts entirely of rayon; where they did, it was usually as a substitute for silk in a parlor or bed throw. While the Lancaster Amish did make all-rayon quilts, it is my feeling that a relatively small number were produced: they are not, in the end, as satisfying to the eye or hand as wool quilts. I think, however, I like them better than most people do; while their format is traditional, the aggressive visual effects of the rayon, so different from the elegant color schemes of the fine wools, take us quickly forward to a post-World War II aesthetic.

The wools were, aesthetically, a particularly fortuitous development in Amish quilt making. These unpatterned materials in the deep, saturated colors the Amish preferred—colors with the same intensities that appear in nature unpatterned—give Lancaster Amish quilts their distinctive inner glow; they absorb and reflect light very differently from other materials, their surfaces are more diffuse, and, unlike cotton quilts, they can absorb a great deal of light without washing out visually; under heavy lighting, in fact, their colors become richer and deeper.

Just as in their adoptions of earlier quilt formats, it would appear that in using these ravishing tones the conservative Amish were continuing clothing color preferences of earlier times. In 1845 Phebe Gibbons, daughter of a Philadelphia Quaker and wife of Dr. Joseph Gibbons, took up residence in Bird in Hand, Pennsylvania in Lancaster County. Her reminiscences of Pennsylvania German life, that of her neighbors, and her keen observations of their customs were published in 1875, and include specific descriptions of her interactions with "plain" people, including a quilting attended by Mennonite women. She mentions showing them her wools: "I displayed my new alpaca, and my dyed merino…" (Gibbons 1872, 33-35). As do women everywhere interested in material and sewing, they shared the enjoyment of examining and discussing fabric. She made some important direct observations of Amish women. In 1872 she saw some at a railroad station; one had a "gray shawl…brown stuff dress, purple apron. One young girl wore a bright-brown sun bonnet, a green dress, and a light blue apron" (ibid.).

In one essay, "An Amish Meeting," Gibbons reported, "The women whom I have sometimes seen with a bright-purple apron, and orange neckerchief, or some other striking bit of color, were now more soberly arrayed in plain white caps without ruffle or border, and white neckerchiefs, though occasionally a cap or kerchief was black" (ibid.). She describes the striking and vibrant colors we associate with classic Lancaster Amish quilts; see, for example, the Bars quilt (CAT. 6), a truly ravishing creation and as close as one can get in proportion and color harmony to a balanced perfection).

Lancaster quilt colors—hot magentas, blues, greens, red—are often startling, an erotic spectrum, especially when we consider those choices in relation to the subdued living patterns of the Amish. Such strong colors in wool materials in fact, however, precede the nineteenth century and aniline dyes; they are to be found in the eighteenth century (one sees them in the calamanco quilts) and perhaps earlier. Coincidentally, Gibbon's observations were published about the time of the first serious Amish ventures into quilt making.

It is not known which of the six most common early Lancaster Amish pieced quilt designs followed the Center Square or if, in fact, they did not arrive at the same time. My attempt at a chronological assessment of this design development is based solely on my dating of the Lancaster Amish quilts I have seen, and is obviously subject to error in both concept and particulars. I suspect, however, that the next of the common designs to appear was the one we call Bars (see the Bars quilt, CAT. 4) which, like the other Amish format, was most likely an adoption of a basic quilt type, the

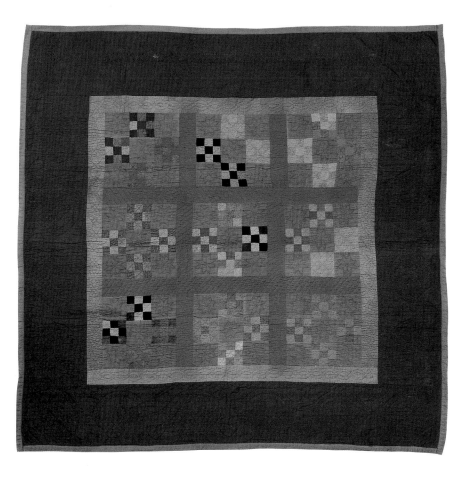

46. Double Nine Patch Variation

Maker unknown, 1925-1935
Amish, Lancaster County, Pennsylvania

Wool and cotton, 177.2 x 177.8 cm
Quilting patterns: eight-point stars, cables, baskets of fruit, hearts, scallops

Tietze & Hodosh Collection

47 (OPPOSITE). *Fans in a Drunkard's Path*

Maker unknown, ca. 1915
Amish, Pennsylvania

Wool, cotton, and cotton sateen,
181.6 x 195.6 cm
Quilting patterns: feathers and
interlocking ovals

The artist embellished the outline of the
Fan motif with embroidery.

Tietze & Hodosh Collection

Pub. Bishop, Robert Charles and Elizabeth Safanda,
*A Gallery of Amish Quilts: Divine Diversity from
a Plain People*, New York, E.P. Dutton, 1976, 59,
Fig. 83.

strip, "strippy," or "columnar" quilt. This was a traditional quilt which could be quickly produced. In the first half of the nineteenth century, some were made by American and English quilt makers to take design advantage of the vertically oriented "floral strip" and architectural "pillar" (column) designs in English chintzes (FIG. 45). Columnar quilts were simply the columns cut from chintzes and pieced together in rows alternating with vertical stripes of the floral strip chintzes to give the effect of architecture in a landscape, or vertical bands of a floral strip chintz alternating with another chintz. Also, strippy quilts of common materials in a vertical format were made in the north of England and Wales, and it is possible some came with settlers to Pennsylvania. This type, sometimes in bright, contrasting plain colors very similar in design idea to the Amish Bars quilts, was common in Pennsylvania both before and after the advent of aniline dyed cottons.

The Center Diamond design, the third and perhaps most common of the six standard early formats, may have appeared about the same time, or perhaps a little later than the Bars (see the Diamond quilt, CAT. 7). This pattern seems to me clearly a retention in schematic form of the late eighteenth- to early nineteenth-century quilt design called in the literature a Framed Center or Center Medallion. The design has a central square design field or a diamond on point within a square, with wide outer borders, and usually square corner blocks. The framed center design was made in both England and the U.S., here usually as a high-style quilt, using fine chintzes and calicoes and often with broderie perse or other embellishments. Sometimes in England it is found in a folksier mode. It remained in vogue in Great Britain and is made there still, but was superseded in America by the development of the block style quilt, and is now made in the U.S. only as a revival design.

While sources other than this have been suggested for this basic Amish format,[3] one support for my contention is that these usually sizeable early framed center quilts (some were the largest American quilts ever made, as big as 10' x 10') tended more toward the square than the rectangular, and were often actually square, in comparison to later quilts, most of which were rectangular; these changes reflect changing tastes in bed dimensions. Classic Lancaster Amish quilts were also most often square, or nearly so, a shape they retained into the twentieth century, long after other quilt makers had turned almost entirely to rectangular quilts. Ironically, the largest contemporary American bed, the "king" size—"which king?" one wonders—is square, so contemporary quilt makers are again making quilts in the size and shape of our early high-style quilts.

The Amish handling of the design eliminated its fussiness and emphasized its very pleasing basic format. For me the Lancaster Diamond is perhaps the supreme triumph of traditional Amish quilt design, and it is certainly among the aesthetic Olympians of all American quilt types. In proportion, balance, harmony, efficacy of color combinations, dignity, and the power to move, none tops it.

The fourth design, which I believe had a contemporaneous origin with the first Diamonds, is called Sawtooth and is just that: a bold diamond in the center of the quilt made with a Sawtooth edge (see the Sawtooth Diamond quilt, CAT. 11). The Sawtooth, built from triangles in a clever strip form, was a basic design device in American quilts. It appeared first in borders, then (as were other pieced border elements from early quilts) was later used in larger scale as a design element on a central field. It exists in non-Amish quilts both in a "bars" or columnar form, vertical bars with

sawtooth edges standing in a contrasting color on a single color field, and in the large central diamond form seen in Lancaster Amish quilts.

The fifth design, Irish Chain, appears to me to be contemporaneous with Sawtooth quilts (see the Irish Chain quilt, CAT. 17). Here the Amish borrowed a very early traditional and popular design made by American quilters in all parts of the country and, as they did with all such borrowings, transformed it through the use of aesthetic devices they had themselves invented. In a typical Irish Chain quilt made by the non-Amish, lines of small linked squares working across a white surface have an expansive quality. As the Amish transformed it, the files are compressed within heavy borders; this gives to the design a drama usually lacking in its typical non-Amish manifestation.

The sixth design, which I feel quite certain was the last to emerge, is what is called Sunshine and Shadow in its Amish version (CAT. 18). The design was made by other quilt makers, particularly in Pennsylvania, where it was also called "Trip Around the World." It is one of a type of ancient designs in which the top grows one piece at a time, without organizing blocks or other devices to break it into component parts; one starts at a convenient point (usually the middle) and works with an ever-growing textile. The earliest patchwork recorded was done in this manner, and the method is still used. It is simple; one needs only a number of squares or hexagons of the same size to assemble it. Sometimes it was organized by quilt makers around a color theme; at its most complex it became Baby Blocks or Tumbling Blocks with a three-dimensional effect. The Amish chose to use the method in a unique manner, building waves of color expanding from a single central square in alternating files of light and dark or hot and cool colors, the whole contained in a strong frame, like a fusion chamber. These basic designs were rendered in an overall format that was varied by using elements from a standard design kit that had these parts and particulars: The quilts were almost invariably more square than rectangular; there was always a central square field framed by wide borders, and often a thinner inner border in a contrasting color. The outer borders could be continuous and of one color, or large square corner blocks in a contrasting color were added. A further optional refinement, when an inner border was used, was the placement of smaller blocks at its corners. All of the features noted here can be seen in the Diamond quilt, CAT. 9.

Any of the six designs and almost all those that followed could be made without corner blocks, in which case they are said by collectors to "float," as in a Floating Diamond (see the Diamond quilt,

48. Ohio Stars

Maker unknown, 1920-1930
Amish, Ohio

Cotton and flannel, 197.45 x 177.8 cm
Quilting pattern: intersecting ovals

Tietze & Hodosh Collection

CAT. 7). There is always an applied outer edging in a color contrasting with that of the wide main border to which it was attached. Some early American quilts had applied woven tape edges; most later quilts were edged by turning the top material over the back or the back over the front, or by using a separate strip of fabric laid over the edge and sewn down on both sides. This last was the Lancaster Amish method, but no other quilt makers employed it exactly as they did. Their edgings extend beyond the body of the quilt rather than ending evenly with its outer edge; they were a consistent, distinct element in the design kit. A further difference between these Amish edgings and those used on other American quilts was their unusual width, sometimes over two inches. They gave, in effect, a finishing "frame" to the design and, combined with the simple, large color fields, the look of contemporary abstract painting. This is one of the reasons modern art collectors so easily integrated Amish quilts into their collections.

Just as the great American invention of the repeated square block as a work method determined the basic design form of the majority of later American quilts, so this Amish "parts kit" approach determined the form of most Amish quilts. The block style and the Amish kit were, in my opinion, the two most important formatting devices invented by American quilt makers. I cannot state with any certainty whether the Amish approach was an ingenious adoption from the block style idea, or an independent invention. Did Amish quilt makers observe and understand the utility of the block style as a work method, and apply it to their initial basic formatting ideas? If one considers, for instance, hundreds of Lancaster Amish Central Diamond quilts almost identical in size, all largely square, with only slight design variations creating their often astounding visual differences, it is not hard to think of them as quilt blocks. Certainly, the working truth at the heart of the block style method, one that applied equally to square quilts, is that it is the easiest geometric format for which one can design, and within which one can make and assemble elements. It was also, strangely, a very American approach to vernacular design, building a form from its essential parts without elaboration. Further, the Amish could see a second truth: The square shape gives at the start a very pleasing visual symmetry. In any case, the retention of earlier forms was a trait of Amish quilt makers in general, and could be attributed to their oft-stated belief in the desirability of continuing to do things as they had been done by those who came before.

From their quilt design kit a body of simple, easy to sew formats was developed, large in scale and composed entirely of squares and rectangles. Accepted and used by most Amish quilt makers, in time these formats became the orthodox patterns, and one assumes that beginning Amish quilt makers would use them. This kit gave the Lancaster Amish great flexibility in creating variations on accepted designs. The use of large, unpatterned pieces created instant color fields; striking design variations could be wrought through contrasting color juxtapositions. This remarkable design device allowed them to create finished quilts of the highest individuality within "acceptable" standard formats, thus satisfying both the community's desire for conformity and individual creative desires. One need only compare Diamond quilts CATS. 7 and 9 and Figure 44 to understand the efficacy of the device.

The Amish understanding of the creative possibilities inherent in the manipulation of color and form variations within set formats is among the most interesting aesthetic discoveries made by American quilt makers. I have in other places pointed out the remarkable similarity of this invention to the later investigations of the same phenomenon by such painters as Albers (in his "Homage to the Square" series, for instance, as noted in Holstein 1973, 114). The method's constraints were, paradoxically, liberating, and from it emerged their cohesive and compelling body of work. While Kraybill (in this volume) notes that "expressions of folk art have bubbled out of Amish life over the centuries," it was really only in their quilts that the Amish made a unique and distinguished contribution to America's artistic heritage. An interesting comparison may be made to the furniture—their greatest design expression—of the Shakers, who chose also to live plainly, only among their own kind, and apart from the world. Lancaster Amish quilts are aesthetically to other American quilts as Shaker furniture is to other American furniture.

We must not overlook in this study the role of the individual artist. The design kit did not appear spontaneously; as happens in other cultures, highly creative individuals developed it, and others adopted it. If the first remarkable happening in the history of Amish quilt making was that they began at all, the second, following closely upon it, was that they developed a design method that satisfied both creator and community.

As the Lancaster Amish involvement with quilt making progressed, the design repertoire matured. They left behind whole-cloth quilts (which continued to be made, however, in conservative jurisdictions in the Midwest) and the Bars design, but added more designs adopted from their neighbors, a number from block-style work, Nine Patch (FIG. 46), and Baskets, the latter made only in one family, according to Herr (in this volume). They began late to make the paramount Victorian busywork style, the Crazy quilt, but tamed it to their liking by incorporating it in a block form which was perhaps the most beautiful manifestation of the design idea in American quilt making (see the Crazy quilt, CAT. 2). Other adoptions from late Victorian decorative styles were Fans (FIG. 47) and the Log Cabin block, a design form the Amish practiced with consummate artistry; see CAT. 23, a Log Cabin quilt that radiates light and energy like a supernova. Always, forms they adopted were put within the overall design framework the Amish had developed, a consistent approach in consonance with their cultural character.

While it is natural to concentrate, in an aesthetic evaluation, on the striking color designs of Lancaster Amish quilts, their less visible quilting designs are of equal importance in any analysis of the quilts' aesthetic and cultural significance. American quilting patterns evolved from the simple to the more complex. In the eighteenth century, most English and American quilts, even high-style show quilts, had quilting which would in later eras be considered crude. The patterns were usually not very complex, often a plain grid in the center and clamshell or some other simple design on the borders, both probably borrowed from styles of quilting seen in earlier imported Eastern quilts. Quilting became more complex in design, and often more florid, in the nineteenth century. As the Victorian period bloomed and decayed, quilting, as did most design, became fussier and more complex. Lancaster Amish quilting designs followed this general trend though its progression, as in other things among the Amish, occurred later. Earlier Lancaster quilts have predominantly geometric quilting designs, large areas rendered in a diamond grid, for instance, with simple figurative elements such as stylized feathers in the borders. As Amish quilt design matured, designs became more complex. More figurative elements appear, simple at first—feathered wreaths and vines in borders, an eight-pointed squared star in the center, hearts, and whirligigs; these designs are part of a

49 (OPPOSITE). Star of Bethlehem

Maker unknown, ca. 1925
Amish, Ohio

Cotton, 231.8 x 233 cm
Quilting patterns: feathers and feather wreaths

Tietze & Hodosh Collection

50. Hole in the Barn Door

Maker unknown, 1930-1940
Amish, Ohio

Cotton, 229.9 x 182.9 cm
Quilting patterns: pumpkin seeds,
diagonal parallel lines, flowers

Tietze & Hodosh Collection

51 (OPPOSITE). Ocean Waves

Maker unknown, ca. 1930
Amish, Holmes County, Ohio

Cotton, 228.6 x 203.2 cm
Quilting patterns: chevrons, diagonal
parallel lines, cables

Tietze & Hodosh Collection

Pennsylvania folk art vocabulary used by many different groups. Flowers of several varieties appeared later, first roses and tulips, then rosa rugosa, and flower baskets. Quilting became fancier, more "Victorian," with that era's penchant for mixed images. All through the classic period, however, Lancaster Amish quilting was invariably fine, and often superb. Their quilting is as significant a hallmark of Lancaster Amish quilts as their colors and large pieces.

It is possible that the very large pieced parts of most Lancaster Amish quilts, which we praise as an aesthetic achievement, were a strategy to avoid the appearance of pride; a top of such large pieces could be quickly assembled on a machine (as they invariably were), thus avoiding the temptation of involved piecing work done either by hand or machine. Speaking of the sewing machine, Granick (1989, 45) points out, "The Amish appear to have accepted this new technology as rapidly as their neighbors. Even the earliest Amish-pieced quilt tops from the 1870s and 1880s were sewn together entirely on the treadle sewing machine." (The sewing machine was clearly the sort of other-culture invention that did not threaten Amish values; the quilt, perhaps, was less certain, so might have taken more time for adoption.) A quilt made with large pieces, with no blocks to assemble, could go from inception to quilting frame quickly. Of course, the top was then embellished with superb hand quilting, but this was less conspicuous than intricate piecing. Certainly quilting at a frame within families and among friends became a major source of enjoyment and group activity, the latter always a plus for Amish women.

I would not want to leave my discussion of Lancaster quilts without pointing out one from this collection I have not mentioned but which I find particularly moving: the serene and perfectly realized Sunshine and Shadow quilt (CAT. 20) which is the epitome of the classic Lancaster County creation.

What was happening during this classic period in other areas of Amish habitation? The Big Valley of Mifflin County in the center of Pennsylvania shelters a number of Amish and Mennonite groups whose theological positions range from the most liberal to the most conservative (the latter represented by the "Nebraska" Amish). Amish settled in the Big Valley in the eighteenth century, and some went on from there to the Midwest. Some Mifflin County quilts exhibit stylistic links both to Lancaster County and Midwestern Amish design traditions. Many used the Lancaster County idea of a standardized design format, with a few changes: Lancaster County quilts tend to be square, Mifflin County and Midwestern quilts rectangular; the latter two use thinner bindings and a variety of materials, with cotton predominating in the twentieth century.

Additionally, the wide range of colors used by groups of differing conservatism in the Big Valley

mirrors developments in the Midwest. The most conservative group favored a "limited palette of traditional 'natural' colors: browns, blues, darker purples, black, darker greens, yellow, ochre, tan and some darker reds" while other groups favored "brighter, 'synthetic' colors" (Granick 1989, 89); compare the Ohio Stars quilt (FIG. 48) and the Star of Bethlehem quilt (FIG. 49). By "natural," Granick means pre-aniline tonalities that conservative Amish groups continued to prefer even after the advent of aniline dyes.

The format of an inner border enclosing a pieced block field became the most important in the Midwest (see the Ohio Hole in the Barn Door quilt, FIG. 50) and it is reasonable to speculate that Mifflin County was the place where Lancaster styles were modified, and from which the new form was sent on. Granick (ibid., 101) observes, "Just as Lancaster County was a 'mother' community to Mifflin County in the 18th and early 19th centuries, Mifflin County in turn became the 'mother' community for new settlements in western Pennsylvania, Ohio and further west." Among favorite patterns were variations on Four and Nine Patch designs. These were the only designs allowed quilt makers of the most conservative of the Big Valley groups, the Nebraska Amish. A number of other patterns were used by less conservative groups, some shared with Lancaster County, some seen mostly in Mifflin County and the Midwest.

While there are clear thematic and stylistic links among all Amish quilts, it may be generally useful to think of the quilts of Lancaster County and its immediate satellites as representing one of the two great visual traditions, and those of Mifflin County and all other areas the second. For convenience I will call the first the Lancaster tradition, and the second the Midwestern tradition.

Ohio and Indiana are the major Amish population centers outside Pennsylvania, but quilts in the Midwestern tradition were made also by Amish living in Illinois, Iowa, Kansas, and Oklahoma. While we can discern in their basic structures forms derived from the Lancaster tradition, and in their specific features concerns shared among all Amish, a distinctive and original aesthetic very different from the parent tradition developed. An uninformed observer would probably not realize both types had been made by a largely homogeneous people. It is not surprising, given the widely varied circumstances of Midwestern Amish life, that quilt making attitudes ranged from the most conservative (those who made only whole cloth quilts) to quite liberal (others very adventurous in design innovation). Common characteristics among Midwestern quilts included the following: the use of unpatterned wool and cotton in early quilts, but cotton almost exclusively starting in the twentieth century; the use of a very broad palette; a rectangular shape; the commonly used inner border format described previously; and an innovative refiguring of pieced block designs.

52 (OPPOSITE). Nine Patch Variation

Maker unknown, 1920-1930
Amish, Ohio

Cotton, 188 x 163.2 cm
Quilting patterns: diamonds
and oval leaves

Tietze & Hodosh Collection

53. Nine Patch

Made by Mary Raber, ca. 1925
Amish, Holmes County, Ohio

Cotton and cotton sateen, 201.9 x 161.9 cm
Quilting patterns: parallel lines,
crosshatching, trailing leaves, cables

Tietze & Hodosh Collection

54. Strip Star

Maker unknown, 1925-1935
Amish, Iowa

Cotton, 216.5 x 158.1 cm
Quilting patterns: double diamonds,
flowers, ropes, cables

Tietze & Hodosh Collection

55 (OPPOSITE). Chinese coins

Made by Mrs. John A. (Barbara) Yoder,
1930
Amish, Oklahoma

Wool, cotton, rayon, 238.8 x 184.2 cm
Quilting patterns: cables and fans

Tietze & Hodosh Collection

Quilts appeared earlier in Midwestern Amish inventories than in the earliest ones found so far in Pennsylvania (1831 as compared to 1836): "Though quilts do not appear in Amish estate papers with the same frequency as they appear in the inventories of non-German families in Ohio, they do appear more frequently than in Pennsylvania Amish documents" (Granick 1989, 106). Unfortunately, Midwestern Amish quilts of the last decades of the nineteenth century are even rarer than those of the Lancaster Amish, so we have little on which to build theories of their design development. Moreover, it is not certain whether quilts were made first by the Amish of Pennsylvania or the Midwest. For a variety of reasons (the Amish settled first in Pennsylvania; Pennsylvania Amish quilts achieved public recognition first and have been more widely studied, publicized and published than those of the Midwestern Amish), it has somehow been generally assumed that the Amish quilt making tradition began in Pennsylvania. But given that it started late among the Amish in general, it could also have begun among, say, the Amish in Ohio. A case might even be made that it was more likely to begin in the Midwest than Pennsylvania, and currently known early dated examples do not necessarily favor the latter. My instincts and some design analysis persuade me at this point that Pennsylvania was first; more documented early material must be discovered and a great deal more research done, however, before any final conclusions can be drawn.

If we review again briefly the two early plain cloth cotton quilts discussed earlier, we find one dated 1849 from Mifflin County, Pennsylvania, and another dated 1869, found in Indiana but thought to have originated in Lancaster County. I add to the list a quilt in my collection that seems almost certain to be Midwestern; it is dated 1898 and is made of purple whole cloth cotton with a black binding. Its quilting patterns (cable border and block-style interior quilting) are very similar to the 1849 quilt. It had a verifiable Midwestern history at the time of purchase, and it is unlikely that a purple cotton whole cloth quilt with a thin edging would have been made in Lancaster County at that date. Thus we likely have examples of plain cloth quilts from Lancaster County, the Midwest, and Mifflin County, the last a place where the two influences apparently mingled. In these early whole cloth quilts we are most likely seeing the same design origins for Midwestern Amish quilts as for those of Lancaster County. Granick (1989, 31) observes, "The few extant examples, the written record and modern prohibitions on pieced designs, which still exist in a few communities, all suggest that simple, one color designs were the first type of Amish quilts."

From the whole cloth quilt and an idea from the Lancaster kit, there developed—most likely in Ohio—an elegant design unique to the Midwestern Amish: a whole cloth quilt with a thin single or double inner border in a contrasting color (see the Single Inner Border quilt, CAT. 64). While the basic design appears to be an early Lancaster Center Square quilt pulled into a rectangle, it

differs from most of those in that the wide outer border, defined in these quilts by the narrow inner border, is of the same color as the inner field; in a Lancaster quilt, the wide outer border would normally be of a different color. Such an overall format, with a single inner border and a field using a repeated, pieced, block-style design, became the most important basic Midwestern pattern, made in all Midwestern Amish areas. It may be thought of as the Midwestern equivalent of the Lancaster County Center Square quilt, the basic platform on which were later mounted new design ideas.

Ohio Amish quilts exhibit some specific characteristics. Early examples used a fairly conservative color range in "old fashioned" tonalities (see the Streak of Lightning or Bricks quilt, CAT. 48). Later quilts (post-1920) employed the wide range of bright colors that had become available by then. During this later period there developed one of Ohio's most significant contributions to the Amish quilt vocabulary, an uncharacteristic use of a black background, unique in American quilts except as it is sometimes found in silk Victorian fancy quilts or parlor throws (see, for example, the Shoo Fly quilt, CAT. 43, which would not have seemed out of place in a painting of the seventeenth-century Spanish Court). Granick (1989, 164) suggests, "The increased use of black, particularly as a background, would seem to be influenced by Victorian sensibilities." These often extraordinary black quilts (see CAT. 42, a Bear's Paw) should be seen as the confluence of three factors: the Ohio Amish's preferred use of fine cotton sateens, which give an appealing luminosity to the quilts in which they were used, the availability of these materials in a wide range of colors in both strong and recessive tonalities, and the decision to set pieced blocks using these often jewel-like tones against

56. Tumbling Blocks

Maker unknown, 1930-1940
Amish, Ohio

Cotton, 223.5 x 193.7 cm
Quilting patterns: cables and leaves

Tietze & Hodosh Collection

a black background. It was a brilliant design concept, and from it came some of the most powerful manifestations of the Midwestern style.

Quilts using small pieced patterns and black backgrounds often produce the sparkling visual effects of modern stained glass (see, for instance, the Stars variant quilt, CAT. 55). Others employ another invention, the use of black sashes so wide they become roads. (One manifestation of this design is, in fact, called Railroad Crossing.) This idea may have developed in Mifflin County (Granick [1989, 39] showed a 1906 Mifflin County cotton quilt with a red field, a fairly wide black inner border and a strong black cross centered within the field and connecting at all four sides). But it was among the Ohio Amish that it was brought to its most powerful statement.

Another characteristic and effective device was the use of a limited palette. The simplest manifestation of this was the two-color quilt, typically a block pattern in one color set against a background of another. In the Bow Tie quilt, CAT. 52, the maker had the brio to turn one block and change the mid-strip in the block above it, touches that turn a pleasant, ordered surface into an enigmatic and arresting statement. Who knows why she did it? Some will no doubt invoke the quilt makers' occasional custom of intentionally building an imperfection into an otherwise flawless quilt so as not to rival God's perfection. I have seen unmistakable evidence of the custom in a few quilts, and so know that it was occasionally done. The issue for me, however, is less intent than result; we cannot know the former, but we can see, and have opinions about, the latter. Having decided for some reason to do this, the maker studied her design, then worked this change at a perfect place, where it would be most noticeable, and perhaps most mysterious. The device of limiting the color range in the quilt refines the statement, emphasizing the integrity and increasing the impact of the visual forms; the same device is employed in Lancaster Amish quilts.

Ohio Amish quilt makers adopted a wide variety of pieced designs used by non-Amish quilt makers. These were often transmuted, however, through sashing, configuration, orientation and color invention, to novel and distinctive statements (see, for example, the great Ocean Waves quilt, FIG. 51, with its luscious color invention—California Dreamin'—and the Lady of the Lake, CAT. 41, with its wonderful Depression Era green background, a defining inner border formed of tics of intense color, and light and dark blocks that look like a flock of displaying exotic birds). I am compelled to mention a few others: the Nine Patch variations (FIG. 52 and CAT. 46), which have to a remarkable degree the aesthetic of Japanese indigo-dyed folk textiles, and the Fans quilt (CAT. 44), which inherited an image captured in Western decorative art during its intense late-Victorian flirtation with things Japonaise, and which an Amish quilt maker flipped this way and that to make a jammed and extraordinary abstract surface; the Nine Patch (FIG. 53), which writes the book on what to do with leftovers; the Baskets quilt (CAT. 38) made the year of the Stock Market Crash with a design like Assyrian grape clusters and an inner border that solves the pink problem; and the One Patch (CAT. 54) Paul Klee that answers the question, "What do those things mean?"

The Indiana Amish shared many stylistic predilections with their compatriots in Ohio and other Midwestern states. In such matters as patterns, fabric and color choices, and sizes, the quilts of different Midwestern Amish groups may be difficult to tell apart. Speaking of the quilts of LaGrange and Elkhart Counties, Indiana, Granick (1989, 123) says, "The majority…were like those made in other Midwestern communities: various block designs created by the arrangement of square and triangular pieces. Among some of the most popular patterns were Shoofly and Nine-Patch variations, Rolling Stone, Baskets, Bow Ties, Swallow Tail, Variable Stars, Double T and Hole in the Barn Door." She also points out that Fans was a popular pattern in Indiana (ibid.) (CAT. 70). On some of the quilts one can see the Victorian-style fancy stitching that was adopted by the Amish after it had been abandoned by other American quilt makers. In color choices Indiana quilt makers followed the general Ohio pattern, a limited range of old fashioned colors in early quilts, and a brighter palette as time went on and choices increased. (For an instructive comparison, see the Ohio Baskets quilt, CAT. 38, which, though made of cotton, uses "traditional" tonalities associated with early wool quilts, and the quilt of the same pattern from Indiana, CAT. 73, which was made in the tonalities we associate with the favored cottons of twentieth-century Midwestern quilts. The two also make a quick study of the visual variety different quilt makers achieved using the same basic designs). Just as black became a favored background color in Ohio, blue was much liked in Indiana, especially in indigo tonalities, a link with the past (see the Hole in the Barn Door quilt, CAT. 72). They also liked a strong red.

In other Midwestern states, the pattern was generally the same as in Ohio and Indiana. Each, however, had some practices which were more particular to it, an indication of the diversity of taste and philosophy among different Amish groups. In Iowa, for example, white was used as a background in association with pastel colors, as in the Star quilt (FIG. 54). Granick (1989, 141) notes the use of unusual borders or piecing arrangements in Arthur, Illinois quilts (see the early Illinois quilt with an atypical and very effective arrangement of Roman stripes, CAT. 69). In other Midwestern states such as Kansas and Oklahoma where the Amish settled later, the rigors and demands of homesteading allowed less of the leisure time, economic resources, and energy innovative quilt making demands. As a consequence, notes Granick (ibid., 144), "For the most part, traditions were brought from other communities and no truly indigenous style developed." Nevertheless, some striking quilts were produced there. The Oklahoma-made Chinese Coins quilt (FIG. 55) is an example of a pattern and format used also in other Midwestern states, rendered here with a end-bar device that strengthens the columns of color bars.

In areas of the Midwest where economics allowed leisure time for making fine quilts, their quilting can be very elaborate and beautifully accomplished; it was perhaps best in the early whole cloth quilts where the main decoration was in the quilting patterns. Fine quilting is normally a sign of an early Midwestern Amish quilt. Midwestern quilt makers did not in general, however, give as much time to fine quilting as did the Amish of Lancaster. Granick (ibid., 111) suggests their fine handwork was given instead to piecing. It must be noted, however, that the Midwestern Amish use of pieced blocks as the main motif in most quilts eliminates the large, open, unseamed fields available to Lancaster Amish quilt makers. These large areas fairly demand fine quilted patterns; and where such areas were available to Midwestern quilt makers, as in the wide, plain borders of their quilts, fine quilting in traditional patterns can sometimes be found.

A comparison of the two great aesthetic traditions, those of Lancaster County and the Midwest, reveals similarities and differences in concept, style, and impact. Basic to both regions was an initial borrowing of craft and design from non-Amish with whom they were in contact; see the startlingly similar Fans quilts from Pennsylvania (FIG. 47) and Indiana (CAT. 70). Equally basic was the transformation of these designs to a statement representative of the Amish spirit. Both regions concentrated almost entirely on making pieced quilts, which use straight lines in their designs, rejecting the major decorative category of American quilts, those employing appliqué technique, whose designs are mostly floral and curved. The Amish made very few quilts which employed appliqué, in keeping with their inbuilt caution about fanciful decoration. Other similarities can be seen in the tendency to employ standardized formats and to build overall designs from an accepted design kit; compare the Sunshine and Shadow quilts from Pennsylvania (CAT. 18) and Ohio (CAT. 53). Another similarity is the use of a limited palette (compare the Sawtooth Diamond quilt, CAT. 10, and the Tumbling Blocks quilt, FIG. 56) and a predilection for an overall dark or somber format enlivened by color, as in the Diamond quilt (CAT. 7) and the Stars quilt (FIG. 48). There was the use of unpatterned materials and a distinctive binding in a contrasting color. A wide outer border and a contrasting inner border were used to define the major design field, as can be seen in the Lancaster

57 (OPPOSITE). Improved Nine Patch

Maker unknown, 1910-1920
Amish, Ohio

Cotton, 201.9 x 165.1 cm
Quilting patterns: vertical parallel lines, zigzag lines, ovals, flowers

Tietze & Hodosh Collection

58. Triple Irish Chain

Maker unknown, 1920-1930
Amish, Lancaster County, Pennsylvania

Wool and cotton, 210.8 x 212.2 cm
Quilting patterns: feather wreaths,
crosshatching, flowers, waffles, feather
plumes

Tietze & Hodosh Collection

County Double Nine Patch quilt (FIG. 46) and the Ohio Nine Patch quilt (FIG. 57). Wools were used in the Midwest only in the earlier quilts, whereas the quilt makers of Lancaster used them until they were no longer available. Quilt makers tended to use favored designs, in some cases over several generations, rather than adopt new ones; see for instance the Tumbling Block quilts from Pennsylvania (CAT. 21) and Ohio (FIG. 56). Fine quilting was used in appropriate areas, with an emphasis on color invention.

A major difference was the divergence in material choices—the eventual Midwestern use of cotton rather than wool—which worked dramatic visual differences among quilts of the two groups; see, for instance, the Irish Chain quilts from Lancaster County, Pennsylvania (FIG. 58) and Holmes County, Ohio (CAT. 47). A stronger pieced-block tradition existed in the Midwest, with the consequent use of smaller design elements. Midwestern quilters used considerably narrower binding, and adopted a much wider range of designs and colors than those accepted and used by the Lancaster Amish. In general, the latter stayed more aloof from mainstream American quilting traditions; their attitudes remained more "traditional." Lancaster quilts were rarely busy; Midwestern quilts range from the restrained control of simple linked squares on solid color backgrounds, as in the Single Irish Chain quilt (FIG. 59), to very active and intricate surfaces, as in the strange Strip Patch quilt (CAT. 32) that took either two years or ten minutes to arrange.

Some of the differences between quilts of the two areas may be accounted for by historical developments. A good deal of the migration to the Midwest from Pennsylvania took place before the advent of Amish quilt making, so the migrants did not carry a developed quilt design tradition there. Additionally, Amish migrating to the Midwest from Europe would not have been exposed to the eighteenth- and early nineteenth-century English and American styles that influenced the Pennsylvania Amish. Amish in the Midwest had more contact with people from dissimilar backgrounds than did their compatriots in Pennsylvania, who lived in close proximity to other Germanic plain people, the Quakers, and so forth. The neighbors of the Midwestern Amish, the non-Amish who had also moved there, brought with them the developing quilt traditions of America, particularly the block style, which influenced their quilt making more than it did that of the Lancaster Amish. While the latter were exposed in Pennsylvania to the new styles, they had developed one on their own that satisfied them, and were slow to adopt design innovations. Some Midwestern quilts, as we have seen, exhibited at least at the beginning more Pennsylvania Amish than non-Amish influence.

As might have been expected, attitudes towards change were often more liberal in the more prosperous and longer-established communities in such places as Lancaster County, Pennsylvania and Elkhart and LaGrange Counties in Indiana. Granick (1989, 129) reports:

> The occasional use of printed fabrics in otherwise solid-colored quilts illustrates the latitude and boundary stretching permitted in most Amish communities. Although the standards called for solid-colored materials, some women apparently felt that a slight bending of the rules was permissible. In certain communities the standards for quiltmaking were formal and strict. In the Elkhart and LaGrange settlements the rules were less clearly defined. The regulations existed, but the women in this large, stable and prosperous community were free to choose from a wide variety of patterns and colors.

Prosperity, in other words, can encourage liberalism. Granick (ibid., 139) writes:

> Every Amish community achieves varying degrees of stability, both economic, and social. Often the two elements are closely linked, and they directly affect quiltmaking.... In communities where religious and social dissensions were strong, quiltmaking appears to have been less an arena for personal expression or artistic experimentation and more a standardized form.

It is important to remember that strong ties have always been maintained by Amish in the Midwest to their brethren in Pennsylvania; there is significant social interaction, and quilt makers of all backgrounds carry their styles with them. Occasionally one sees a Lancaster format reproduced in cotton in the Midwest, and block patterns popular in Mifflin County or the Midwest made in

Lancaster County; see the Bars quilt from Ohio (FIG. 60) and the Double Nine Patch from Pennsylvania executed in a very Midwestern layout (FIG. 46). It is quite possible that the Lancaster Amish adoption of such pieced block patterns as the Nine Patch was influenced by Midwestern practices; one must be aware, however, that the chronology of these designs among different Amish groups is very sketchy at this point, and awaits further research. In this collection is a very early and unusual Lancaster Amish quilt using Nine Patch blocks in a Bars format (CAT. 13), which may point to Lancaster County as the progenitor of the earliest block pattern adoptions; the prototypes for such designs, as for all classic Lancaster Amish patterns, exist in earlier non-Amish quilts (FIG. 61). It must also be remembered that, while they may differ widely in the details of their lives, the basic Amish tenets of belief and practice are consistent group-to-group, Pennsylvania to the Midwest and beyond. The application of this constancy to quilt making over a long period thus produced aesthetically integrated bodies of work remarkable for their consistency and quality. We can see in their quilts, as in that of no other American quilt making groups, an unintentional collective endeavor in which generations of Amish women applied their creative energies to the same basic design ideas. This produced a body of work of great importance to our social history because it carries within it documentation of technological and historical changes in American life. It is also of equal importance to our aesthetic record, as we can observe in it the evolution of design experimentation within very tight parameters by a singular, largely homogeneous group of creators over a very long period.

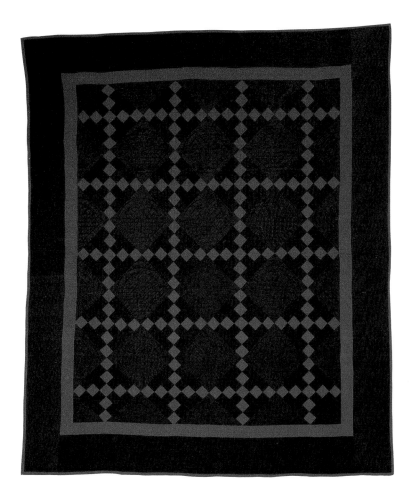

59. Single Irish Chain

Maker unknown, 1920-1930
Amish, Holmes County, Ohio

Cotton and cotton sateen, 226.1 x 191.8 cm
Quilting patterns: parallel lines, baskets of fruit, interlocking ovals, ropes

Tietze & Hodosh Collection

It seems clear that the creation of these remarkable textiles was a peculiar cultural event in Amish history. The dangers of worldly involvement were evident at the start: regarding the earliest Amish quilt discussed here (1849), Granick (1989, 30) wrote that the quilting patterns mimic "pieced blockwork in its placement and design." The maker of that progenitorial quilt was clearly aware of the stylistic developments in American quilts, what was current at the time she adopted this anachronistic whole cloth format, and she displayed her knowledge by putting it, however inconspicuously, onto this plain canvas. Was not this pride in and display of knowledge antithetical to the Amish spirit? Did it not push things a bit? Thus we can see at the very beginning of their involvement an attitude both consistent and inconsistent with their world view. It was consistent in that they adopted something of interest and utility from the larger culture, choosing as their aesthetic model a "tried-and-true" format no longer in fashion. This is what one would have expected, as the Amish are slow to adopt foreign elements into their culture and have no interest in being fashionably in step with the times. (They have, after all, retained for ideological reasons the clothing, equipment, occupations, work patterns, and many attitudes of an earlier time. In the New England of the 1850s, their beards, hats, and pants would not have looked significantly out of place. As for the sameness—the uniformness of Amish garb—that, too, was somewhat common in an earlier time in rural areas throughout the Western world; most workers in particular areas dressed alike. Even now, one can travel through agricultural areas of Europe where the indigo blue cotton pants, shirts, and jackets of farmers are like a uniform. The horse drawn equipment moving across the Amish landscape is what one would have seen on any prosperous American farm before the advent of tractors. In other words, they are particularly noticeable now by contrast with their neighbors, but the contrast would have been largely insignificant in the last century.)

The opening of the Amish culture to quilt making appears culturally inconsistent when we consider they had the choice of adopting the craft to make utilitarian quilts (of which they did make many) exclusively. Instead, they chose at the beginning and thereafter to also make quilts of expensive materials, and to quilt them finely. They had, in fact, access to their traditional New World bedding of choice, woven coverlets, so a change was not necessary (except, perhaps, if coverlets became more expensive as fewer weavers made them, and utilitarian quilts were a good economic alternative). They did not make their fine quilts as warm bed covers, and the quilts did not initially fulfill a practical need in Amish culture. In making them, the Amish used resources that might have been devoted to more practical concerns. Quilt making carries a strong scent of worldly pride and vanity. I have pointed out the powerful Amish social mechanisms arrayed against such potentially disruptive endeavors. How, then, did they rationalize joining this questionable undertaking?

The Amish relationship to the singular expression of the creative impetus is clearly ambivalent. Everywhere one looks in Amish culture there is evidence of a basic discomfort with individual achievement, with standing out; yet there are areas where achievement and status are discreetly recognized. A good illustration of the dilemma can be found in a letter, cited in Pellman (1985, 26) to a Mennonite magazine, *Family Life*, which the Amish read:

> After making a new organdy covering for one of the little girls, I had it lying on the ironing board all ironed nicely and ready to wear. She admired it awhile then asked if she could try it on. So I put it on her. She gently ran her hand along the back, then asked, "Mom, does it look like a cake from the back?" In her eyes a neatly rounded covering made her think of cake. I could tell she was proud of such a covering. Burning with shame on the inside, I wondered why I had spent so much time in making it so nice and round if that was sowing seeds of pride in her heart. Where can we draw the line between neatness and pride?"

Could anything more neatly describe the Amish dilemma? In our culture, creativity is honored for its own sake, and much aberrant, antisocial, self-gratifying, wildly nonconformist behavior by artists is tolerated. In Amish society, the creation of beautiful things must always carry with it potential moral difficulties. The reason for this is simple: that abhorred pride, which can lead one away from God (see Kraybill's discussion of pride, in this volume).

Granick (1989, 31) notes that an Old Order Mennonite woman from Pennsylvania "stated quite emphatically in an interview that cutting up material and sewing it together again was 'just for pride.'" In another section, Granick (ibid., 145) observes:

> In every Amish community, as among any group of people, there have always been men and women who exhibited visual, intellectual or artistic skills which surpassed the normal standards. Such skills are not highly valued or even particularly encouraged in Amish culture. In some communities the expression of these talents is even vigorously discouraged.

Equally, however, we have evidence of an accommodation to such desires and their expression; the personal expression of a creative drive is not completely foreign to the Amish, as Kraybill (in this volume) notes: "Bending to the call of community…does not smother individual expression. Outside observers are often surprised by the amount of individual freedom within the boundaries of Amish society." As we have seen, Amish women chose to make textiles which were not simply utilitarian, but which used the finest materials, some of which were bought specifically for quilt making. Granick (1989, 89) states: "Purchasing goods specifically for making quilts…was a common practice among Amish women throughout the United States. In the Nebraska Amish community, however, this was generally less acceptable and women relied heavily on the leftovers from their sewing work." This tradition does not mean the latter did not make fine quilts, simply that the buying of material only to make quilts violated their sense of propriety. Elsewhere Granick (ibid., 128) notes:

> In contrast to some other communities, quilts in Indiana often included a strong red. In the Elkhart and LaGrange communities, women purchased this bright red specifically for quiltmaking. The color was not permissible for dresses.

Further proof, were it needed, lies both in what we know about Amish culture, and in what their quilts tell us. The Amish could have continued to make whole cloth quilts, as some Amish groups have. They could have treated quilts as they do, for instance, their buggies, made in a form similar for all but with touches (the color of the buggy's top, for instance) changing according to the tastes of different groups. Instead, we see in their quilts a clear evolution in form and color; we see quilt makers taking advantage of changes in materials and available palette; we see them sorting patterns available to them in the surrounding culture, and picking those most suitable to their circumstances and taste; we see in Amish quilt making, in short, all of the exploitation of circumstance we see in the creative work of any culture. And had the quilt makers not been able to gain tacit approval within their culture for this activity, Amish quilt design would not have evolved.

What else accounts for the seeming exceptions made for quilts, their special or "protected" status? Quilts appear to have occupied a unique position in the lives of many Amish, and in the sensibilities of many Amish groups. First, unlike the buggies mentioned above, quilts are not key objects in Amish self-identification, the hats, clothes, conveyances, etc., that signal to the outside world the Amish intention to remain separate. The maintenance of such identifying objects' visual integrity, a time freezing, is important to the maintenance of the Amish self-image. Quilts were not among that sacred group, so once accepted they could develop stylistically.

Quilt making, because it allowed so many more tempting opportunities for individual expression, probably became one of the "permissible" creative activities that came closest to the edge of impropriety, encouraging pride. Given what we know about Amish attitudes, and what we can see in their quilts, it was clear that women pushed the possibilities of the craft to that edge, relying on their finely-honed perception of what could be done without incurring group disapproval. We can see in their quilt making evolved strategies that allow the quilt maker to meet the demands of custom and orthodoxy, and at the same time fulfill creative urges and give an individual stamp to her work.

The communal aspects of quilting most likely helped in its acceptance by the Amish: one could elect to focus on the quilting bee itself rather than the single creative woman piecing her materials. Such cooperative work ventures are an integral part of Amish life, embodying an ideal mix of social contact, communal action, recreation, and meaningful work, thus few rationalizations would be necessary to adopt it as an acceptable custom. We should also remember that Phebe Gibbons (1872) described a quilting she had attended in Lancaster County a decade before that. It was attended by both "the 'world's people'" and Mennonite women (she describes their "clear-starched Mennist caps"), indicating that there likely existed at that time the sort of easy social intercourse one expects in an informal rural society, an exchange that happens with less ease now.

Equally, we have the desire of individuals to create. "Women in Lancaster purchased the finest quality fabrics for their quilts, arranged their choices of colors and designs with great care and then lavished hundreds of hours and yards of thread on their quilting'…" (Granick 1990, 17). Amish women had the same love of fine fabrics as other Americans. Herr (in this volume) quotes a "Morgantown quilt maker" reminiscing about buying fabric from a peddler in the 1940s:

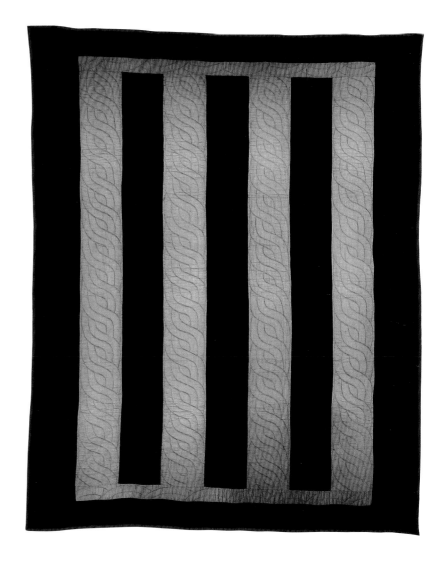

60. Bars

Maker unknown, 1920-1930
Amish, Ohio

Cotton and cotton sateen, 188.6 x 153 cm
Quilting patterns: diagonal crosshatching, cables, fans

Tietze & Hodosh Collection

And Romaine crepe! That was a fabric! It started to come in when I was a teenager. And whoever had a Romaine crepe dress that following season, man, they were top, on top of the mountain!

Hostetler (1974, 18-19), discussing the Amish woman's role, notes, "For her satisfaction in life she turns to brightly colored flowers in the garden and in her house in the winter, to rug-making and embroidery work on quilts, pillowcases and towels, and to shelves full of colored dishes in her corner cupboard. These are her prized possessions, some the work of her hands, made not for commercial gain, but for the enjoyment of the household and her host of relatives. She adds beauty to life with quilts, rugs and flowers." It seems clear from accounts I have noted here, and others known to me, that quilt making served Amish women of the late nineteenth and twentieth centuries as it did their "English" sisters: for both, it was an important outlet for creativity.

Amish society, which has an egalitarian thrust, shuns conspicuous status-seeking. Yet there are ways of acquiring it. Status can be earned, for instance, by scrupulous adherence to orthodoxy, or conferred by being raised (or having one's husband raised) to a position of church leadership. Paradoxically, as regards quilts, both taste and quilt making skills could accumulate status. Herr (in this volume) notes that "subtle choices of fabric for clothing and quilts among the Lancaster County Amish reflect a great deal about the individual's status within the community."[4] She quotes a quilt maker in her 60s who was once Amish: "Your quilt reflected a lot on you, if your quilts had expensive material.... You are much put in categories by the way you keep your house, by the kind of material, the kind of stitches you do in your sewing...." Amish women of the speaker's generation judged each others' skills and aesthetic choices in quilt making just as did other American craftswomen, and positive judgements conferred status. Again, Herr quotes the quilt maker: "They took an awful lot of pride in the [quilt making]. That pretty well set the stage for which category you fall into, as far as ability and workmanship. It was very much a part of you.... The kind of material, the stitching and of course the patterns, colors."[5]

In Amish society as in others, high status members have greater latitude for experimentation (Granick 1989, 160):

> Innovation plays an important role in the Amish community and the personal character of the innovator has a great deal to do with whether the innovation is deemed too radical or threatening, and therefore unacceptable. If the wife of a bishop in a community institutes a small change in the use of different fabrics or the use of a new pattern, it may then be judged acceptable for other community members. In many communities, any woman whose place in the church is well established and who generally follows all the important rules is able to try something a bit different in the realm of quiltmaking.

Thus we can see a mechanism through which Amish quilt design could evolve in a culture wary of change.

It would also appear that quilts themselves became status objects among the Amish. We have seen that special materials were purchased to make them, and that much time was spent in their quilting. Almost all folk cultures have status textiles, and they are often used ceremonially. By "status" textiles I mean those that are made within the culture or are luxury imports, require significant resources to make or acquire, and have important symbolic meaning or use within the culture. Status textiles where they exist in a culture are almost always involved in rites of passage—birth, coming of age, marriage, and death—and quilts are no exception; they are, in fact, especially potent in this regard as they are associated in the most intimate manner with the bed, shelter and witness to the human dramas that unfold there. One indication of their significance to the Amish is that they were used as coverings for a guest's bed (Granick 1989, 155). This is important as it shows that the Amish used a status textile for display, at once honoring a guest and showing the female skills of the family. It is clear they had sentimental value, even for a people who do not prize sentimentality. Herr (in this volume) quotes a 68-year-old former Amish woman who, in describing a quilt

61. Strip Quilt with Four Patch Blocks

ca. 1840
Non-Amish, Northeast

Chintzes and calicoes, 243.8 x 213.4 cm

Such early pieced styles were no doubt the inspiration for the first Amish designs incorporating pieced blocks. See, for comparison, the Lancaster Amish Nine Patch Blocks in a Bars format quilt, CAT. 13.

America Hurrah, NYC

she received as a girl and saved but never used, said, "I guess it has become more of a part of me than I realized."[6] Status textiles, which embody family and community history, are, as is true for this one, often put away "and never used," that is, not used up. Rather, they are often passed down through generations, and it is in the act of preserving them, and in their role thus to recount history between generations, that they are used; that is often the intended "use" of status textiles from the beginning, even though they may be in a utilitarian form.

It was my personal experience, when we were actively collecting Amish quilts and were privileged occasionally to be able to collect their histories directly, that each older quilt's history was known and significant to the quilt's owners. It was, in fact, because of their quilts' significance to the Lancaster Amish that so many made during the classic period were preserved.

Did quilts and quilting have significant symbolic content for the Amish? In a number of ways, their uses mirrored "English" custom. In this century the Amish adopted the custom of giving friendship quilts to women leaving the community; they also made them as fund raisers for worthwhile causes (Granick 1989, 155); see the Lancaster County Friendship quilt (CAT. I). The quilts have other functions, however, which seem to me of even more importance. Particular significance lies in the quilts' association with weddings. Hostetler (1974, 161-62), discussing dowries, notes, "All mothers by tradition make a few quilts and comforters for each child. These are usually made years in advance so they will be ready when needed. One housewife made three quilts and two comforters for each child; she had seven boys and three girls." Granick (1989, 155) notes that quilts had been used for gifts among the Amish since the nineteenth century, adding that they were traditionally made for sons and daughters as part of their wedding portion, as well as for babies and children. These symbolic uses are indicative of the importance of marriage, procreation, children, and large and fertile families to the maintenance of Amish culture. Herr (in this volume) notes the significance of quiltings to Amish women, illustrated in an interview with Miriam Stoltzfus, who remembered her days as a young Amish woman: "Quilts said a lot to the community. If you were busy quilting this said you were going to get married. It was an honor to be invited to a quilting because…that would give you self-confidence, you're able to quilt now. You wanted to be a good quilter." She went on to say that quilting was an art to which every girl was exposed and that it was a must to learn how to piece and quilt. The Amish took from American culture the use of quilts as utilitarian objects, which one might have expected if such quilts were more practical or economical than woven blankets, but the Amish also understood and took for their use the quilts' function as symbolic and status textiles.

May we look deeper? May we legitimately find intrinsic in the quilts' aesthetic, rather than their uses, symbolism specific to Amish concerns? Were there built into the quilts' compelling forms—consciously and unconsciously—reflections of the Amish spirit? Where status textiles are made within the culture that uses them, expensive raw materials are usually used in their composition, the utmost care attends their production, and the designs are expressive of the culture's deepest and clearest beliefs and concerns. I have mentioned how such factors as the economics and attitudes of different Amish communities shaped the way their quilts looked. And it is clear that the triumphant "plainness" of their quilts is a reflection of the emphasis on plainness, a foreswearing of showiness in their lives. I wish here to look more closely at the aesthetic of Lancaster Amish quilts in relation to their world view and preoccupations.

As we have seen, obedience to God's will is a basic tenet of Amish belief. In their biblically-centered view, there is a careful order in God's creation and His rules for us. God established His hierarchy of earthly creation with man at the pinnacle, and woman as his helpmate. They believe the words of Genesis. "God created Adam and Eve to 'replenish the earth, and subdue it and have dominion over…every living thing that moveth upon the earth.' In the same way, man's highest place in the universe today is to care for the things of creation" (Hostetler 1975, 67). "The account of Creation and the parables in the Bible inform the Amish that they must be stewards of the soil…. The Amish believe that with good management the land will not only yield a livelihood, but, as in the Garden of Eden, their farms should reflect pleasantness and orderliness" (Hostetler 1989, 56). Man was given the world as his habitation and he is its caretaker; careful husbandry, a reflection by man of God's caring for the earth and His people, both fulfills God's will and ensures the fertility and continuance of Amish life. The careful organization of the Amish farm, as well as their social and religious practices, reflect this view. The means to sustain life comes from the soil, the Amish man's fields and the Amish woman's gardens. "The Amish housewife is responsible for the appearance of the yard and garden and spends many hours trimming and grooming it. Brilliant banks of flowers… glow against the white buildings; often the flower beds are arranged in neat geometric formations, scrupulously tended to keep their shape" (Safanda and Bishop 1976, 12). In creating an ordered environment man disciplines himself to follow God's will. Thus the ordered Amish farm is a fitting symbol of their sense of their place in Creation. In ordered and carefully tended fields and gardens, the freedom and abundance of God's creation can be expressed and flourish.

I think Lancaster Amish women selected, modified, and retained the basic forms of their status (fine wool) quilts not only because they were inherently conservative, but also because the designs were a satisfying graphic reflection of their world view. Many have seen in the careful geometry of their quilts a reflection of carefully tended Amish fields. While too much can certainly be made (and usually is) of such direct visual comparisons, it is clear at a simple level that the restraint and order of Lancaster Amish quilts are a statement and reflection of traits considered desirable in their culture. Granick (1990, 15) says, "The quilts are a visual synthesis of the Amish ideal that spiritual beauty is the result of utmost simplicity, perfect group harmony, and a reverence of tradition." I believe, however, we may look a little further.

One could view an entire exhibition of Lancaster Amish quilts from a distance, receiving the profound impact of their tautly constructed color fields, and observe little if any of their often extraordinary quilting. The observer who had experienced the exhibition in that manner would take away an impression of the unique dynamism of Amish quilts without sensing the significance of the counterpoised quilting patterns. Contained within the hard-edged squares, triangles and rectangles that define the quilts' color surface, are the extraordinary quilted designs. Some are geometric; others spring, as I have noted, from Pennsylvania Germanic culture and are in themselves symbolic: the eight-pointed star, "whirligigs" (also sometimes called "hex signs," a form of cross), hearts, and tulips. These symbols are often contained in small visual boxes such as the corner blocks at the junctions of inside border bars. These little boxes can also contain individual flower heads. The smaller designs are counterpoints to the large scale, flowing, often sinuous and luxuriant motifs, usually floral, found quilted in the large color areas. There can be twisted cables, or grapevines with bunches of grapes and leaves, undulating feather vines or sprays of fiddlehead ferns in the wide outside borders, a feathered wreath surrounding an eight-pointed star or flowers in the center, and flowers—roses, tulips, rosa rugosa—on curving stems quilted on the cover's large-scale sections. Sometimes the works of man and nature are combined in a basket filled with fruits on the borders of the quilt.

These curvilinear forms are the natural motifs set in contrast to the rigid, artificial, straight-edged geometry of the color areas, and are all the more remarkable since Amish quilt makers did not, as we have seen, normally use the curved designs of floral appliqué work in their tops; given their love of flowers, it must have been very tempting. Instead, they put inconspicuously within the spare, precisely organized forms of their quilts—emblematic of a world brought to order by man so God's will can best be served—the fruitful abundance and uncontrollable movement of His creation. Equally, they juxtapose symbolically the sex-differentiated spheres of Amish society, the intellectual structure and order of the Church and the tangible structure of the farm—male domains—dominating the quilt, which is supported and enriched by natural forms emblematic of the garden, the house, fertility—women's spheres. (And it might be noted it is the quilting stitches that hold the structure together.)

We can see in it a symbolic blueprint: the Amish worldly domain and God's plan for His creation. Do we need to debate intent, decide if the makers of these quilts were artists? And could those questions, in fact, be answered? The blueprint, formed by the most fundamental and deeply imbedded cultural dogma of the Amish, is one testified to and supported every day within their society.

Amish women adopted a craft full-blown in another culture, applied their cultural imperatives to their understanding and practice of it, and in so doing created a distinctive body of work that adds to our sense of their separateness. Their society was and is contrary, born in dissension, nourished in disobedience, transplanted of necessity, and flourishing in difference and defiance. Certainly they intended to make the quilts they did, could see that theirs were different. But their quilts were different because their makers were different, not because they set out to make different quilts; their creative energies were directed by a different set of cultural criteria. In our culture, kudos are awarded for innovative work, for surprising and novel changes to a standard or for the invention of completely new forms; the intention is to be or become different. In theirs, the intention is to remain different (from the ever-changing culture around them), and their quilts are a manifestation of this intention rather than an attempt to innovate. Their quilts were innovative by indirection.

Our cultures diverged, and while theirs remains astonishingly stable, ours changes at an ever-accelerating pace. They are active and passive in a manner opposite from us. They actively shun and do not desire the things we want the most. They passively and effectively resist the things we most promote. They are most active in and long most for the things about which we have become most passive. The more they pull away from us, the more we want to be near them.

Each day they must accept and practice the very hard work of being different, of living in a conscious manner; it is consciousness and intention which informs their relationship to the world they choose not to mirror. In their quilts, as in all else they do, we see conscious statements of their differences; through the maintenance of these differences, they bear witness. In their quilts, as in all else they do, they, too, see conscious statements of their own intent; they fashioned from quilts another instrument of memory which, like *Martyrs' Mirror*, sustains their faith.

The Amish made little art because their spirit was turned away from the world to the practice of a conscious life; art is superfluous and distracting baggage for people who are "strangers and pilgrims" in the present world (Hostetler 1974, 50). They seem to us exotic and interesting, and we are perhaps drawn to observe them not for their novelty primarily, but because we recognize at some level the choice their witness offers, that they have preserved a spirituality that once pervaded our culture, that we were once more like them as they are now than as we are now, that we were once, in fact, them; they think more like Buddhists but look more like us. We recognize in the same instant that they are the mythic American rural Golden Age for which we long, and that we could not live there. We left the Garden long ago, and could not now go back; we couldn't do the practice. I think, in the end, we are drawn to the Amish and their quilts because we know so much about modern art and the effluvia of our civilization, but so little about living comfortably, whereas the Amish know nothing of modern art and little of consumerism that they like, but a good deal about living happily in their skins.

For all its constraints, imperfections, and tensions (and there are many), and for all the manifestations of asocial behavior which can be seen among the Amish, as among all people, the Amish have created a more successful culture than ours because its members in general are both spiritually and materially comfortable, because it delivers, it gives its members what it says it will if they do what it asks them to. And the Amish have accomplished and maintained these essential things, without which a culture is a sham and a delusion and a failure, entirely through their own efforts, through mutual aid and support without—from principle—using the social safety mechanisms available to them as citizens of a wealthy and diverse democracy. While the Amish may not exhibit in their personal lives the expressions of romantic love we associate with male-female relationships and family life, we must not assume they do not experience the range of emotions we sustain. Nor should we think that the calm and control, which are for them esteemed traits, manifested by Amish women mean they lack passion and intensity of feeling. We must give them the full triumph—intellectual, aesthetic, and emotional—of their quilts, and not assume our sophisticated perception and explication of the objects gave them their aesthetic life. Since we cannot live in the Amish soul, we have no right to assume we know its boundaries. Archibald MacLeish (1972, 79-86), after a tour of Lancaster County with Lord Snowden in the 1970s, made these observations:

> The usual view of the Amish is that they are an anachronism, a people who got stuck in history back with the horse and wagon and an Old Testament God and other chronological oddities, such as the art of husbandry, and domestic skills long unused, and harmonious lives…. The fact is that the Amish, for whatever reason, had spotted the idea of progress for what it is a long time before the rest of us had learned the cliches—or even learned that they were cliches…. It wasn't technological inventiveness that was going to define the future for the Amish. They themselves would do the defining. And what they would define would be their lives; not the means to life but the life itself…. What the Amish mean is the nature of human life, the living of human life….

Though what MacLeish says is probably in large measure true, does it not sound like a refined rhetoric of the American Golden Age myth? Is that what the Amish now unwittingly invoke? Marc Olshan (1980, 161-162) observed that the Amish have been resented in the twentieth century by rural neighbors looking to "progress" for their salvation. "Frugality and self-sufficiency become vices rather than virtues in the context of a rural community that is aggressively promoting economic growth…where the American dream is still being sought, the Amish may symbolize a slap in the collective face of the community…." But he saw this changing: "In fact, to the extent that goals in American society have become less materialistic or economic in nature and more oriented toward quality-of-life issues, the Amish have been increasingly invoked, either as exemplifying aspects of the good life, or as a potential model to which others will have to turn out of necessity." There it is. By simply sticking stubbornly to principle, the Amish have become classic American culture heros: successful because they are in the main self-reliant, self-sufficient and self-possessed, independent, devout and God-fearing, trusting in Providence and thankful for their blessings, content with simple pleasures and firmly rejective of bad influences, highly principled, willing to sacrifice for their ideals and unwilling to take handouts from anyone including the government, extraordinarily hard working, frugal and respectful of tradition, good and careful as parents, skeptical of the world yet open to joy, hopeful that no one will interfere in their lives and being unwilling from principle to interfere in the lives of others, and rejective of television. As soon as all of this is generally known, someone will almost certainly try to turn Lancaster County into a theme park, Ethical World: "Watch highly motivated people in their traditional clothing apply principle to their daily lives."

62. Bars

ca. 1890

Amish, Lancaster County, Pennsylvania

Wool, 213.4 x 182.9 cm

Collection of the author

People who know nothing of modern art experience in our culture each day the effects of the aesthetic visions of Malevich, Mondrian, Picasso, Lichtenstein…it is the only trickle-down theory that seems to work. In a similar way, Lancaster Amish quilts have pervaded our lives. Designers of chic paraphernalia adopted their colors wholesale once the first exhibitions and books featuring the quilts appeared. The rich, saturated colors—deep reds, greens, purples, grays, and blues that echo the loveliest colors in nature—were perfect, especially as they appear in the combinations seen in Lancaster Amish quilts, for upscale customers vaguely uneasy about an increasingly plastic (and nastily colored) world, customers who were somewhat interested in conservation and very interested in displaying what appeared to be solid values. Some of the catalogs of chic mail order houses have in recent years shown products—briefcases, sweaters, sleeping bags, skirts, flashlights, towels, T-shirts, sheets—and product lines almost entirely informed by Lancaster Amish color schemes. (As far as I know, no credit was ever given the source of this palette. Is anyone surprised?) Thus we have the extraordinary situation of tourists traveling to Lancaster County to observe the Amish, unknowingly sporting on their backpacks, jackets, wallets and other impedimenta, the colors of the heirloom quilts the Amish no longer own, having sold them, once the price got high enough, to help them maintain the life they understand is more important than possessions.

Some have, perhaps legitimately, decried the disappearance of old quilts from Amish communities, but they have probably not talked with many Amish about it. Certainly, it is almost always better, from a standpoint of cultural health, for artifacts to remain with the people who made them.

But when an heirloom quilt could be traded, as some ultimately were, for several acres of the farm a son would need to maintain a family in the Amish way, the choice was easy for them: the pull of their clear priorities was stronger than the tug of sentimentality, and the quilt went on to such carefully assembled collections as the one pictured in this volume. (Ironically, the interest generated by traditional Amish quilts in the "English" world gave great impetus to the now-flourishing Amish quilt-making industry, a significant source of income.) Power does not reside for the Amish in relics, but in the memory, the will to obey, the devoted heart; they have internalized the Creator.

Because Amish quilts are so powerful for me I have waited, perhaps from some misplaced sense of objectivity, until the end of this article to make a few comments about my personal reactions to them. I am, in effect, segregating these comments and stating their subjectivity, hoping that what has come before was more objective. That way I can both reveal some anecdotal material I think the reader may find of interest and give my relatively unencumbered reactions to the quilts without feeling that I have compromised my analyses of them.

The first Amish quilt I ever saw was pivotal in affirming my (then) developing sense of quilts as a distinct phenomenon in American art history. It had been thrown over a bed in a small, seasonal antique shop (open in warm weather) on Route 30 in Pennsylvania; the year was 1969 or 1970. As I remember, its proprietor was a schoolteacher who kept the shop when he could, and the unheated building may itself have once been a small schoolhouse. The bed, which was what he really wanted to sell, was in a bare upstairs room, and the quilt was simply fulfilling one of its traditional functions, covering up the bad looking bits, in this case, a set of bare springs. The quilt was an early, simple, and for us, visually amazing Lancaster Amish Bars quilt in three colors: purple, green, and a red called "pigeon's blood." The colors were individually very evocative, intense, and passionate, different from those I had seen in any other American design form. Their combination was very strange, but had been decided with complete authority. The parts that formed the design, really just a few colored strips on a red field, were perfectly balanced in scale, proportion, and placement, a sense reinforced by the harmonious interactions of their colors. I had never seen anything like it; it seemed at once familiar and foreign, accessible and inaccessible, American and…what?…Japanese?

It was like looking into a place one knew well and discovering that somehow a completely unknown and fully realized art form had appeared there. Had I overlooked it? Where had it come from? What, I thought, did this have to do with beds? What sort of bed, what sort of person, would this have been made to cover? I was completely confounded by it, and remember commenting to my wife, Gail, that we appeared to be looking at a masterpiece created by a deranged angel. The proprietor was disappointed in our lack of interest in the bed, but was nevertheless ultimately happy to sell us the rag that covered it. I believe we might have asked him if he knew anything about it— we usually did when we bought quilts—and he may even had said it was Amish, but if he did, it didn't register. We knew very little about the Amish then; we saw them in their fields, on the roads in their buggies, we came into slight contact with them in general stores and at markets, we bought produce from them at the Lancaster Central Market on Saturdays; we were, in other words, like other tourists.

We put the quilt up on a wall in our New York apartment and looked at it for a few days.

Its large pieces were made of the finest wools we had ever seen in an American quilt, but all of single colors, no prints. The colors were rich and deep, like those of eighteenth-century clothing. The design was confidently and completely realized and the quilting was extraordinary, in patterns we recognized as those of earlier American quilts. We guessed at a date of 1880, though in many ways it seemed older than that. We had been collecting quilts all over Pennsylvania for several years, at shops large and small, and in flea markets, and had never seen anything like it. We assumed that it was a unique and aberrational work of genius. Though we did not know its origin, it seemed clear that it had emerged from America's quilt-making tradition, and it confirmed several important things for me. One was that American quilt makers had not practiced the craft in a received, traditional manner, but had used it to create a body of work with unique design characteristics; that, in fact, the medium had been remarkably liberating, and was in some ways akin to the visual experimentation of some modern art. It confirmed also that there were few limits on the design inventions of American quilt makers. And it encouraged us to continue a "painterly" approach to seeing and collecting quilts.

We lived with the quilt for awhile, and gradually it dawned on me that it must follow a general rule: such complete and fully realized works of art from folk cultures were never, in fact, aberrational, were never single works of genius, did not simply appear from nowhere, always had precedents, parents, ancestors. If, after all of our looking at, collecting, and reading and thinking about Pennsylvania quilts, and after all of our time in the byways of the state talking to people who knew and made quilts, we did not know its lineage, it probably meant we were simply ignorant of it. Such a completely successful work had to be part of some tradition; it just could not have been an isolated phenomenon. Perhaps it had not been made in Pennsylvania, though that seemed unlikely.

What to do was easy enough. On our next collecting trips to Pennsylvania we talked to everyone we could about it. Finally someone we knew who dealt often with the Amish said, "Oh, that's probably an Amish quilt." We asked why we had not seen more of them for sale. She shrugged. "No market," she said. "Not the look anyone's interested in."

Of course, that began a quest, and we were fortunate to have had a little while to build a type collection before the feeding frenzy began, and fortunate enough to have met some Amish who were willing to interact with us in a relaxed manner (a relative rarity, especially then), and to have a chance to observe Amish life not as insiders, certainly, but neither as total outsiders.

We used that first Bars quilt (FIG. 62) in "Abstract Design in American Quilts," an exhibition of 61 pieced quilts we curated for the Whitney Museum of American Art in New York in 1971. And when Jean Lipmann asked us to select one quilt from that show for the comprehensive exhibition, "The Flowering of American Folk Art" curated by her and Alice Winchester for the Whitney in 1974, that Bars quilt was the one we selected. It had been a pivotal work in my understanding of quilts, I knew they would include other great quilts both pieced and appliquéd, and I was anxious that Amish quilts be represented in an exhibition whose purpose was to highlight the pinnacles of American folk art. By the time that exhibition opened, we had been able to study many more Amish quilts, and had perhaps begun to understand them.

Sometime after collectors first began to appreciate Lancaster Amish quilts, antique dealers from the Midwest began to arrive in New York City with quilts that seemed initially as strange as the first Lancaster Amish quilts we had seen; the dealers told us the quilts had been made by Amish living in Ohio and Indiana. We could occasionally see a few similarities between the Midwestern quilts and those made by the Lancaster Amish, but it was clear that a different aesthetic had evolved and developed fully there. The quilts were very different from those of the Pennsylvania Amish, which seemed to me, while "modern" in result, in actuality a distillation of all that was extraordinary in the color and vernacular design of the past several centuries. The Midwestern Amish quilts, while they also carried hints of the past, seemed more "made in America," more rooted in the experience of the later nineteenth and twentieth centuries, more contemporary. Each was a distinct and remarkable body of work, unique chapters in the aesthetic history of American quilt making.

By late 1972 I was confident enough about the importance of Amish quilts to that history to include fifteen illustrations of Lancaster Amish examples and two of Ohio Amish quilts in my second book on quilts, *The Pieced Quilt*, published in 1973. I grouped 13 color plates of Lancaster quilts together and talked about them as a distinct design phenomenon within the tradition of Pennsylvania quilts.[7]

We collected some Midwestern Amish quilts, thought about them, and concluded that many are as remarkable aesthetically as the quilts of Lancaster County. But our hearts had been lost to the latter as to no others, and that added emotional impact always engaged us. We recognized and could eventually analyze and understand the extraordinary accomplishment of American quilt makers. The mental adventure engaged us completely and gave us enormous intellectual satisfaction. Once in a while there would leap from the mass a quilt that equally engaged our minds, hearts, and stomachs, that gave us that lovely rush one gets when confronted with a perfectly realized piece of art, when everything goes off at the same time. Only Amish quilts did that consistently. Opening a stack of them was one hit after another; no matter how many times I had looked at our Amish quilts, and no matter that, after a while, I knew what the front would be like because I recognized the back, they still did it to me. And so, as I wrote this article, I thought about that: Why do Amish quilts so uniquely affect me and others? That, I thought, was a legitimate and appropriate question to address here.

I have pointed out that quilts can engage our attention as do no other artifacts. I do not think I can say it better than I did in an article I wrote for a catalog of another exhibition: "Quilts exert their great force in our minds and imaginations because they combine in single objects so much information of importance to us: the potent congruence of beauty, sentiment, history, utility and significant function (people were born and died under them; they cover our dreams)" (Holstein 1991, 19). It is, of course, a description of poetry, which carries in a distilled and inextricably interwoven manner, our most significant news. And I think that Amish quilts simply do it better than all the others; the data is more compressed, more intense. They are strongly evocative intellectually for me now because I sense in them the weight of a very interesting history, of Pennsylvania's early and extraordinary role in American life, of Amish settlement in the New World after persecutions in the Old, of the movement of Americans west, of our industrial and commercial history, of quilting's great craft tradition. All of that knowledge, however, came after decades of studying and thinking about quilts, long after I saw Amish quilts for the first time. In the beginning there was simply their immense visual power, the aspect that made us interested in quilts in the first place. What, in fact, made them so powerful for me in particular?

First, I liked modern art before I knew anything about quilts. I like it very much, particularly abstract art, particularly the sparer abstract painting and sculpture. The things I value most in the fine arts are the things I like in all the rest, architecture, the decorative arts, music. A powerful structure, form unadorned, powerful fields of color, things with definite edges. Clearly, this made recognizing and appreciating what was going on with quilts an easy task.

Amish quilts, and particularly Lancaster Amish quilts, are the pinnacle of this sort of taste. The colors and surfaces of their woolen materials have a depth and intensity, a kind of veracity denied other fabrics; it is a presence I see more in pre-aniline textiles. Amish quilts look like color samples for designers of battle flags or standards of emerging nations; their colors stir us up. The balance and harmony of the best are extraordinary, the proportions and relations of their various parts are often almost impossibly correct, not just in one quilt, but in one after another; there are simply none that do it better. The great ones achieve a tension and dynamism that make them fairly hum; they are like Zen banners, always active, always in repose. In the best there is no separation of color and form; it comes through as a whole, instantly, the moment of perception for which words and thoughts are superfluous. Such perfect things slip past all of our defenses and strike us directly in the heart. Later on, we make theories about them.

Such power is, of course, the essence of any great work of art of any medium, and I have certainly experienced it, often in more complicated forms, elsewhere. To find it in American quilts was, however, unexpected. And to have so many in a body of work reach that level is extremely rare. In the end I hardly think of these things as quilts. They seem to me more like meditative symbols, pennants for monasteries, and, of course, great paintings. If art is a religion, these quilts are its mandalas.

It is, perhaps, a fitting irony that the major aesthetic works of the American subculture most determined and successful in avoiding the ensnarements of modernity, are in their effects, so extraordinarily modern.

POSTSCRIPT

The day I finished editing this manuscript, our evening paper had a little story about an Amish carpenter on its front page:

CARPENTER REFUSES $212,000 TO PRESERVE SIMPLE LIFESTYLE

An Amish carpenter whose wife died last year after a truck slammed into the family's buggy has turned down a $212,000 insurance settlement because he believes the money could threaten his family's way of life, an attorney says. "I admire him," said David Richie, who was appointed guardian for nine of the family's 11 children. "For the simple fact that he felt the money would cause more problems than it would solve." Mahlon Lambright, 43, of Mondovi in west central Wisconsin near Eau Claire, asked Dunn County Circuit Judge James Wendland on Thursday to dismiss a petition for a wrongful death settlement because he feared his children would not appreciate Amish traditions when they grow up. "He pointed out to the court that members of the Amish community helped him by providing food and clothing and having an auction," Richie said. Lambright told the Judge: "I do feel if I take this money and they found out I got all this money, they would feel bad." Richie said money is not as important to the Amish as the community itself."[8]

NOTES

1. . I have always found it interesting that the group of Americans who most closely resemble the Amish in their equally anachronistic habits of daily dress (many of the men wear vests, long black coats, and wide-brimmed black hats; the women follow specific grooming codes), their use of a language with Germanic content, and their maintenance of a sense of separation from the world are the Hasidic Jews of New York City.

2. From an interview conducted by Patricia Keller with a formerly Amish woman at the Lancaster Heritage Center, Lancaster, Pa., as quoted in Herr (in this volume).

3. Elizabeth Safanda and Robert Bishop, in their *A Gallery of Amish Quilts*, point out that some traditional Amish hymnals, called *Ausbands*, have tooled leather covers with square brass bosses at the corners and a diamond on point in the middle, the basic format of the Diamond quilt; the bosses are sometimes worked in repousse in feather, fan, or floral designs, common Amish quilting motifs. Ausbands are, however, rectangular rather than square.

4. See note 2.

5. Ibid.

6. Ibid.

7. The first books devoted exclusively to Amish quilts appeared in 1976 when Elizabeth Safanda and Robert Bishop's *A Gallery of Amish Quilts: Design Diversity from a Plain People* and Phyllis Hader's *Sunshine and Shadow* were published. A number of others have followed, ranging from the folksy-cum-art to the art-plus-anthropology to the pure art. David Pottinger's *Quilts from the Indiana Amish* and two books by Rachel and Kenneth Pellman, *The World of Amish Quilts* (1984) and *Amish Crib Quilts* (1985), combined many pictures with a little history. Granick's *The Amish Quilt* (1989) was the result of a great deal of original research in Pennsylvania records, among the Amish, in newspapers of the earlier part of the century, etc. *The Art of the Quilt*, a large format, slip-cased, full-press, Japanese-spare art book on the great Lancaster Amish quilts in the Esprit (clothing company) collection had comments by curator Julie Silber and an introduction by the contemporary art critic (*Time* magazine) and author Robert Hughes.

8. "Carpenter refuses $212,000 to preserve simple lifestyle." *Syracuse Herald-Journal* (Syracuse, New York), 11 March 1991:19.

Catalog

AMISH QUILTS
FROM THE COLLECTION OF
CINDY TIETZE & STUART HODOSH

Pennsylvania
Quilts

FRIENDSHIP QUILT

Various names of quilters and dates in embroidery in 63 blocks, 1870-1928
Lancaster County, Pennsylvania

Wool and cotton, 212.1 x 198.1 cm
Quilting pattern: cables

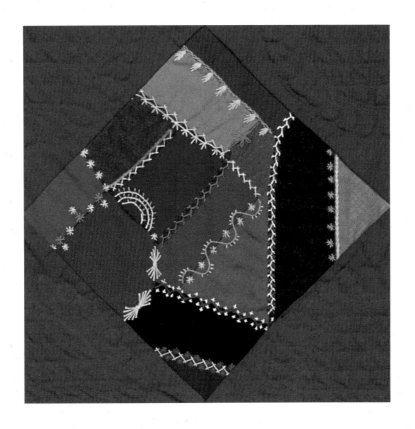

CAT. 2

CONTAINED CRAZY QUILT

Made by Rebecca Stolzfuss, 1912-1922
Lancaster County, Pennsylvania

Wool and cotton, 203.2 x 206.4 cm
Quilting patterns: feather wreaths, crosshatching, grapevines, feather plumes

CAT. 3

BARS

Maker unknown, 1920-1930
Lancaster County, Pennsylvania

Wool and cotton, 184.8 x 165.6 cm
Quilting patterns: feather wreaths, baskets with tulips, crosshatching, scallops

CAT. 4

FLOATING BARS

Maker unknown, 1880-1900
Lancaster County, Pennsylvania

Henrietta wool and cotton, 207 x 175.9 cm
Quilting patterns: crosshatching, diamonds, feather wreaths, feather garlands

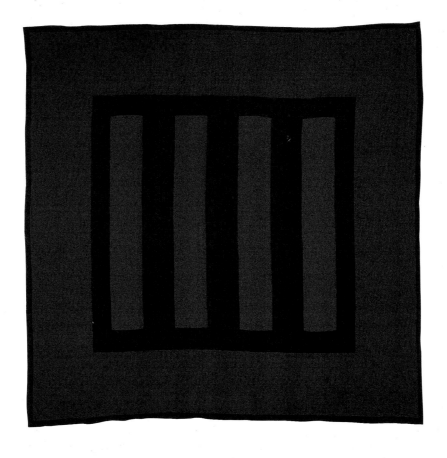

CAT. 5 (ABOVE)

CONTAINED BARS

Maker unknown, made for Aaron Beiler, ca. 1939
Lancaster County, Pennsylvania

Wool and cotton, 212.1 x 215.3 cm
Quilting patterns: crosshatching, cables, baskets, stars, scallops

CAT. 6 (OPPOSITE)

BARS OR STRIPES

Maker unknown, 1920-1930
Lancaster County, Pennsylvania

Wool and cotton, 213.4 x 200.7 cm
Quilting patterns: crosshatching and winding roses

CAT. 7

CENTER DIAMOND

Maker unknown, 1910-1920
Lancaster County, Pennsylvania

Wool and cotton, 191.1 x 194.3 cm
Quilting patterns: feather wreaths, eight-point stars, roses, grapevines, feather garlands

CAT. 8 (ABOVE)

DIAMOND IN A SQUARE

Maker unknown, 1935
Pennsylvania

Cotton, 183.5 x 212.7 cm
Quilting patterns: double concentric feather wreaths,
crosshatching, feather garlands

The artist quilted the initials "AP" and the date "July 6, 1935"
inside the center diamond.

CAT. 9 (OPPOSITE)

DIAMOND IN A SQUARE

Maker unknown, 1920-1930
Lancaster County, Pennsylvania

Wool and cotton sateen, 199.4 x 198.8 cm
Quilting patterns: open roses, feathers, feather wreaths,
eight-point stars

The artist embroidered the initials "D.F." in two identical
sets on opposite corners on the back of the quilt.

CAT. 10 (ABOVE)
Dowry Quilt
SAWTOOTH DIAMOND IN THE SQUARE

Made by the King Sisters, 1920-1930
Lancaster County, Pennsylvania

Rayon and cotton, 210.8 x 213.4 cm
Quilting patterns: Sawtooth, roses, grapevines, feather garlands

The quilt is initialed "EF" in embroidery
on the back corner of the binding.

CAT. 11 (OPPOSITE)
Dowry Quilt
SAWTOOTH DIAMOND IN THE SQUARE

Made by the King Sisters, 1920-1930
Lancaster County, Pennsylvania

Cotton and rayon, 208.3 x 212.1 cm
Quilting patterns: feather garlands, grapevine wreaths, roses

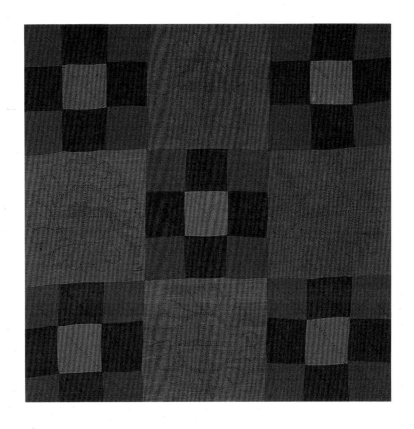

CAT. 12

NINE PATCH VARIATION

Maker unknown, 1910-1920
Lancaster County, Pennsylvania

Wool and cotton, 194.4 x 174 cm
Quilting patterns: feather wreaths, crisscrossing, crosshatching,
grapevines, baskets with hearts

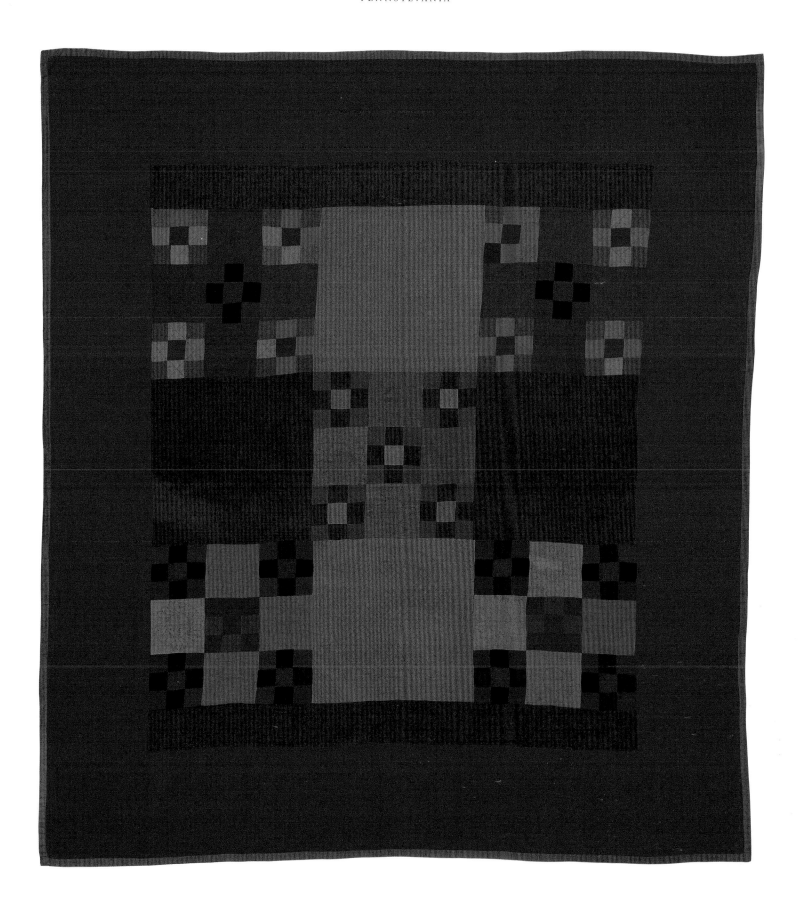

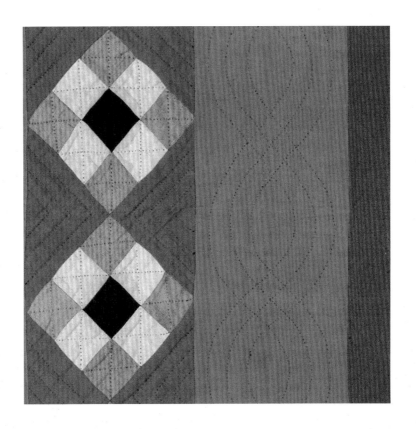

CAT. 13

NINE PATCH IN BARS

Maker unknown, 1900-1910
Lancaster County, Pennsylvania

Wool and cotton, 189.9 x 192.4 cm
Quilting patterns: cables, pinwheels, chevrons, baskets,
"open-floating" hearts, flowers, scallops

Pub. Ed. L. Thomas Frye, *American Quilts: A Handmade Legacy*,
Oakland, The Oakland Museum History Department, 1981, 82.

CAT. 14 (ABOVE)

DOUBLE NINE PATCH

Maker unknown, 1920-1930
Lancaster County, Pennsylvania

Wool and cotton, 221 x 216 cm
Quilting patterns: floral wreaths, floral vines,
crosshatching

CAT. 15 (OPPOSITE)

NINE PATCH VARIATION

Maker unknown, 1930-1940
Lancaster County, Pennsylvania

Wool and cotton, 211.5 x 211.5 cm
Quilting patterns: feather wreaths, crosshatching,
pinwheels, chevrons

CAT. 16

SINGLE IRISH CHAIN

Maker unknown, 1885-1895
Lancaster County, Pennsylvania

Cotton, 195.6 x 194.3 cm
Quilting patterns: crosshatching, leaf wreaths, trailing tulips

The artist embroidered the initials "EF" on a corner on the back of the quilt.
According to the collector's notes, the quilt was made for Elizabeth Fisher,
born April 11, 1879.

CAT. 17

TRIPLE IRISH CHAIN

Made by Sadie Stolzfus, 1915-1925
Lancaster County, Pennsylvania

Wool and cotton, 205.7 x 210.2 cm
Quilting patterns: diamonds, crosshatching, feather wreaths, feather garlands

The artist embroidered the initials "ss" on a corner on the back of the quilt.

CAT. 18

SUNSHINE AND SHADOW OR GRANDMOTHER'S DREAM

Maker unknown, 1920-1930
Lancaster County, Pennsylvania

Wool and cotton, 200.7 x 201.9 cm
Quilting patterns: floral garlands, crosshatching, diamonds

CAT. 19 (ABOVE)

SUNSHINE AND SHADOW OR **GRANDMOTHER'S DREAM**

Maker unknown, 1920-1930
Lancaster County, Pennsylvania

Cotton, 200.7 x 190.5 cm
Quilting patterns: crosshatching, interlocking ovals and scallops,
eight-point stars

CAT. 20 (OPPOSITE)

SUNSHINE AND SHADOW OR **GRANDMOTHER'S DREAM**

Maker unknown, 1925-1935
Lancaster County, Pennsylvania

Wool, wool crepe, rayon, cotton, 211.7 x 205.1 cm
Quilting patterns: crosshatching, flowers,
fruit baskets, fleurs-de-lis

CAT. 21

TUMBLING BLOCKS

Made by Mrs. Enos King, 1910-1920
Lancaster County, Pennsylvania

Wool and cotton, 186.7 x 184.2 cm
Quilting pattern: crosshatching

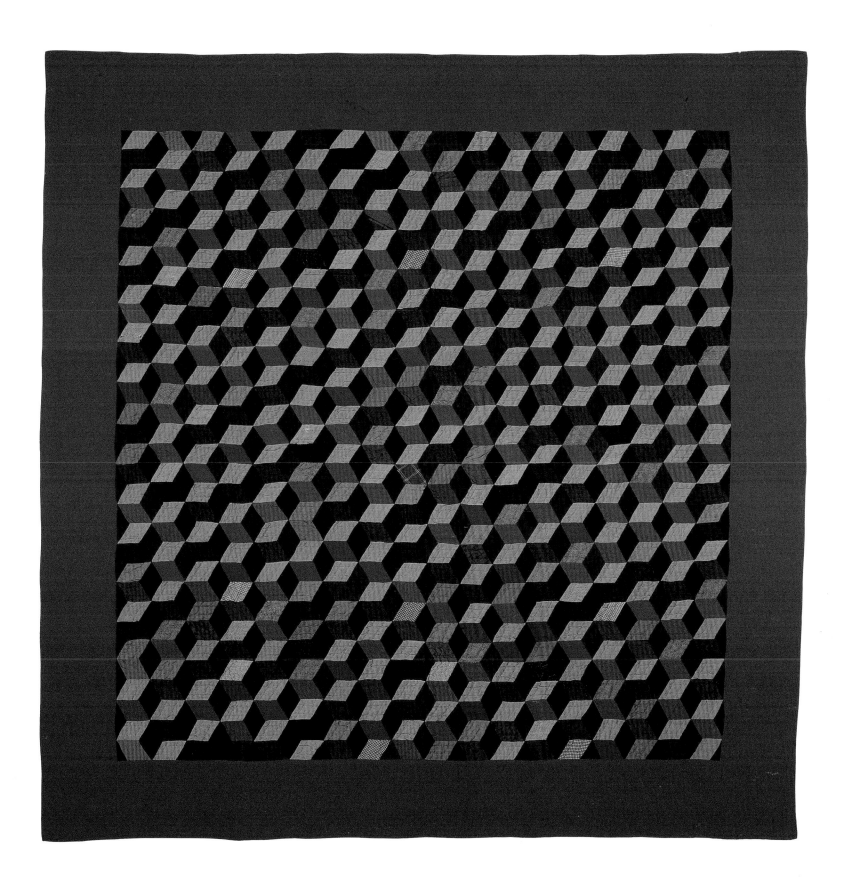

CAT. 22 (ABOVE)

LOG CABIN - LIGHT AND DARK

Maker unknown, 1910-1920
Western Pennsylvania

Cotton and cotton sateen, 190.5 x 183.5 cm
Quilting pattern: concentric squares

CAT. 23 (OPPOSITE)

LOG CABIN - STRAIGHT FURROW

Maker unknown, 1900-1910
Mifflin County, Pennsylvania

Wool and cotton sateen, 194.4 x 168 cm

Pub. Granick, Eve Wheatcroft, *The Amish Quilt*,
Intercourse, Pennsylvania, Good Books, 1989, 92.

CAT. 24

OHIO STARS BURSTING

Maker unknown, 1885
Mifflin County, Pennsylvania

Cotton, 219.1 x 179.7 cm
Quilting patterns: feathers and parallel lines

The artist initialed and dated the quilt "C.Y., 1885 " in embroidery inside the inner square.

CAT. 25

DOUBLE WEDDING RING

Maker unknown, 1940-1955
Lancaster County, Pennsylvania
Cotton, 233.7 x 203.2 cm
Quilting patterns: zigzags, diamonds, waffles

CAT. 26

Crib Quilt
COURT HOUSE STEPS

Maker unknown, 1880-1890
Lancaster County, Pennsylvania

Wool and cotton, 94 x 51.4 cm

CAT. 27

Crib Quilt
STARS

Maker unknown, 1920-1930
Lancaster County, Pennsylvania

Cotton, 111.1 x 95.3 cm
Quilting patterns: diagonal lines, diagonal crosshatching, double parallel lines

CAT. 28

Crib Quilt
BOW TIE

Maker unknown, 1930-1940
Nebraskan group, Mifflin County, Pennsylvania

Cotton and cotton sateen, 102.9 x 90.2 cm
Quilting patterns: double pumpkin seed, vines, leaves

CAT. 29

BASKETS

Maker unknown, 1920-1930
New Willmington, Pennsylvania

Cotton, 210.5 x 189.5 cm
Quilting patterns: leaf, parallel lines, zigzag lines, cables, hearts

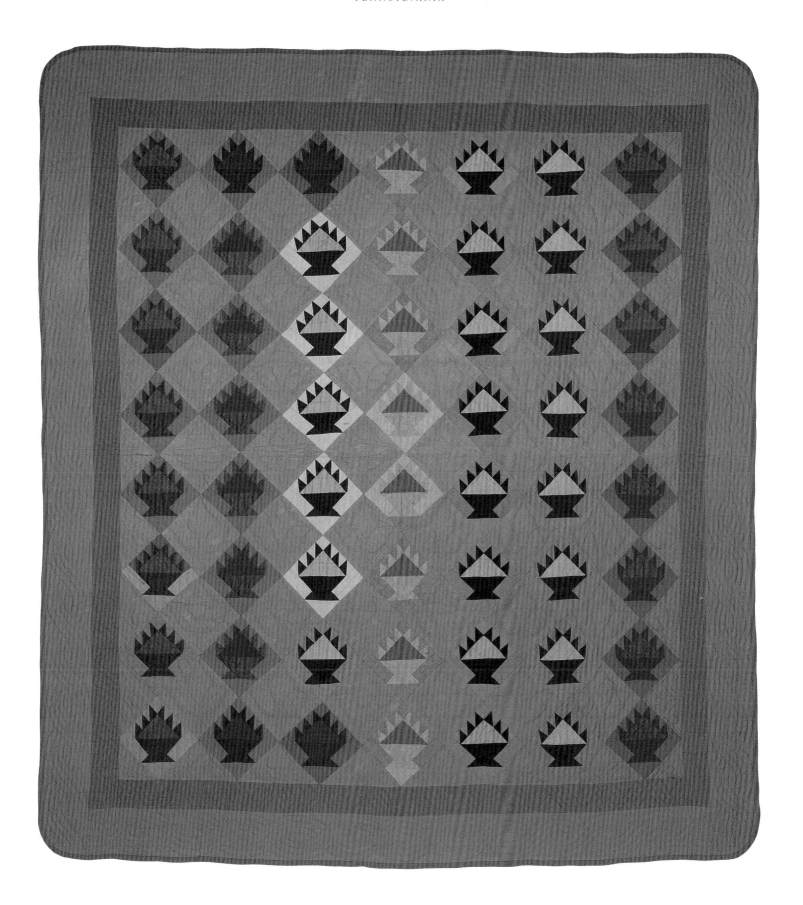

Ohio
Quilts

CAT. 30

TUMBLING BLOCKS

Made by the Smucker Family, 1890-1900
Geauger County, Ohio

Cotton, 221 x 208.2 cm
Quilting patterns: parallel lines, diamonds, double zigzag lines, cables

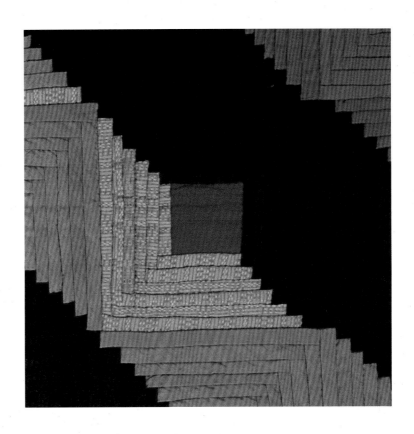

CAT. 31

LOG CABIN - STRAIGHT FURROW

Maker unknown, 1910-1920
Ohio

Wool and cotton, 201.9 x 205.7 cm
Quilting pattern: cables

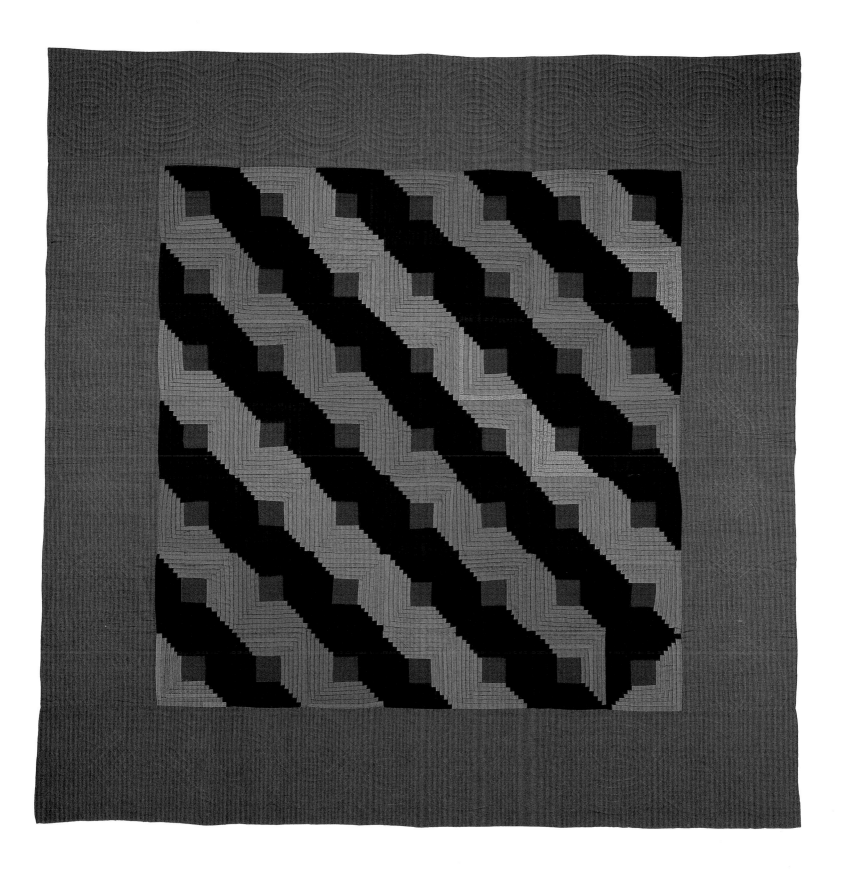

CAT. 32

STRIP PATCH OR LOG CABIN VARIATION

Maker unknown, 1920-1930
Ohio

Cotton, 186.1 x 168.3 cm
Quilting patterns: chevrons and concentric diamonds

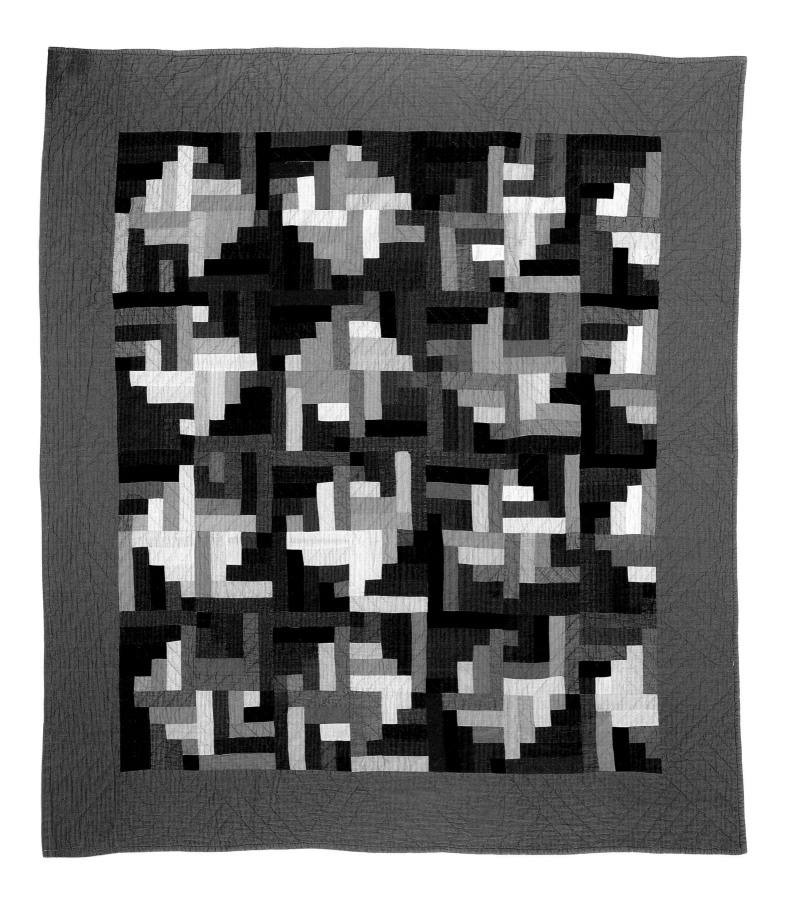

CAT. 33

LOG CABIN - BARN RAISING

Maker unknown, 1925-1935
Ohio

Cotton, 256.5 x 215.9 cm
Quilting pattern: fans

CAT. 34 (ABOVE)

LOG CABIN – BARN RAISING

Maker unknown, 1910-1920
Midwest

Wool, 179.6 x 182.1 cm
Quilting patterns: single squares and single zigzags

CAT. 35

LOG CABIN – BARN RAISING (SIDE ONE, OPPOSITE)
BARS (SIDE TWO, ABOVE)

Maker unknown, ca. 1920s
Holmes County, Ohio

Cotton sateen, 198.8 x 196.2 cm
Quilting pattern: chevrons

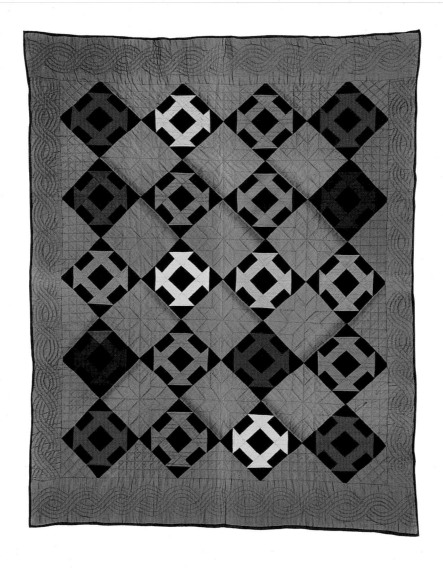

cat. 36 (ABOVE)

HOLE IN THE BARN DOOR OR **MONKEY WRENCH**

Maker unknown, 1925-1935
Ohio

Cotton and cotton sateen, 200.7 x 162.6 cm
Quilting patterns: cables, parallel lines, eight-point stars, crosshatching

CAT. 37 (OPPOSITE)

HOLE IN THE BARN DOOR OR **MONKEY WRENCH**

Maker unknown, 1915-1925
Holmes County, Ohio

Wool, cotton and cotton sateen, 206.4 x 173.4 cm
Quilting patterns: feather wreaths, crosshatching, fans, parallel lines

Pub. Pellman, Rachel and Kenneth, *The World of Amish Quilts*,
Intercourse, Pennslyvania, Good Books, 1984, 94.

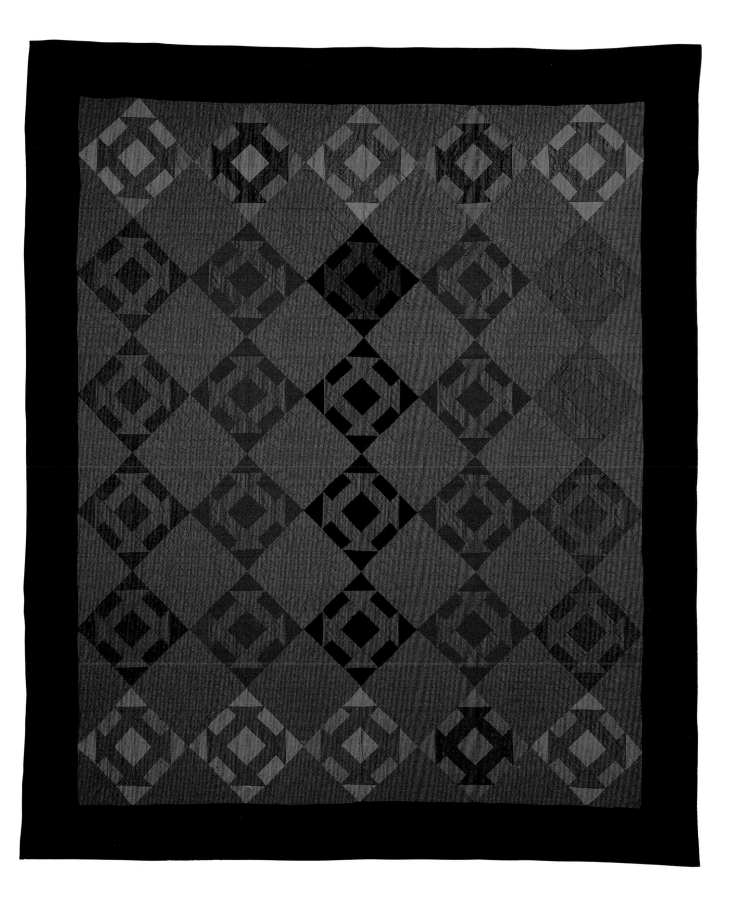

CAT. 38

BASKETS

Maker unknown, 1929
Ohio

Cotton and cotton sateen, 187.3 x 189.2 cm
Quilting patterns: parallel lines, flowers, ropes, double cables

The artist initialed and dated the quilt "L.M., 1929" in embroidery on the corners of the outside border.

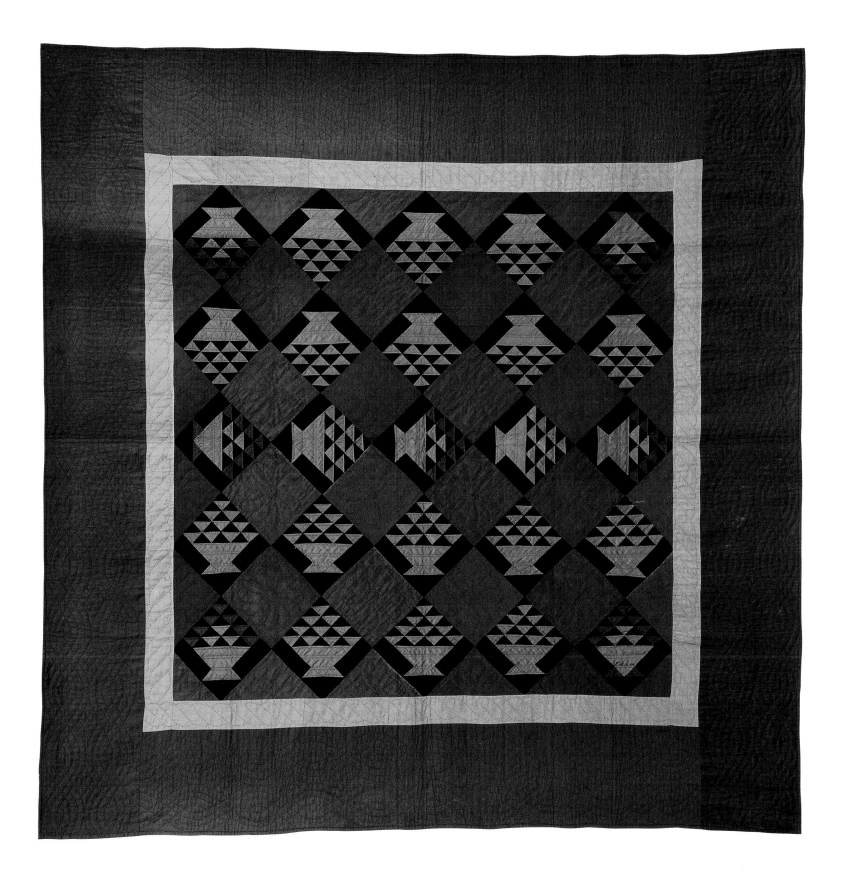

CAT. 39 (ABOVE)

NORTH CAROLINA LILY

Maker unknown, ca. 1920
Ohio

Cotton and cotton sateen, 213.4 x 174. cm
Quilting patterns: feather wreaths, crosshatching, ropes

The artist emphasized the Carolina Lilly pattern
by double quilting the outline of the baskets and the lillies.

CAT. 40 (OPPOSITE)

BASKET OF CHIPS

Maker unknown, 1931
Ohio

Cotton, 151.1 x 191.8 cm
Quilting patterns: flowers, ropes, cables

The artist quilted the date "JAN 1931" inside the center square.

CAT. 41

LADY OF THE LAKE

Maker unknown, 1936
Holmes County, Ohio

Cotton, 175.9 x 207.6 cm
Quilting patterns: cables, chevrons, tulips

The artist dated the quilt "1936" in embroidery on the front.

CAT. 42

BEAR'S PAW

Maker unknown, 1935
Ohio

Cotton and cotton sateen, 208.9 x 170.2 cm
Quilting patterns: crosshatching, feather wreaths, cables, diagonal parallel lines

The artist dated the quilt "1935" in embroidery at the bottom of the inner border.

CAT. 43

SHOO-FLY

Maker unknown, 1920-1930
Ohio

Cotton and cotton sateen, 190.5 x 161.9 cm
Quilting patterns: flowers, triple parallel lines, fiddlehead ferns

CAT. 44

FANS IN STAINED GLASS SQUARES

Maker unknown, 1910-1920
Ohio

Wool and cotton, 179.1 x 179.7 cm
Quilting pattern: crosshatching

CAT. 45 (ABOVE)

NINE PATCH

Maker unknown, 1910-1920
Ohio

Wool and cotton, 210.8 x 157.5 cm
Quilting patterns: cables, concentric squares,
double parallel lines, diagonal lines

CAT. 46 (OPPOSITE)

NINE PATCH OR **IRISH CHAIN**

Maker unknown, 1920-1930
Ohio

Cotton, 152.4 x 195.6 cm
Quilting patterns: flowers and oval leaves

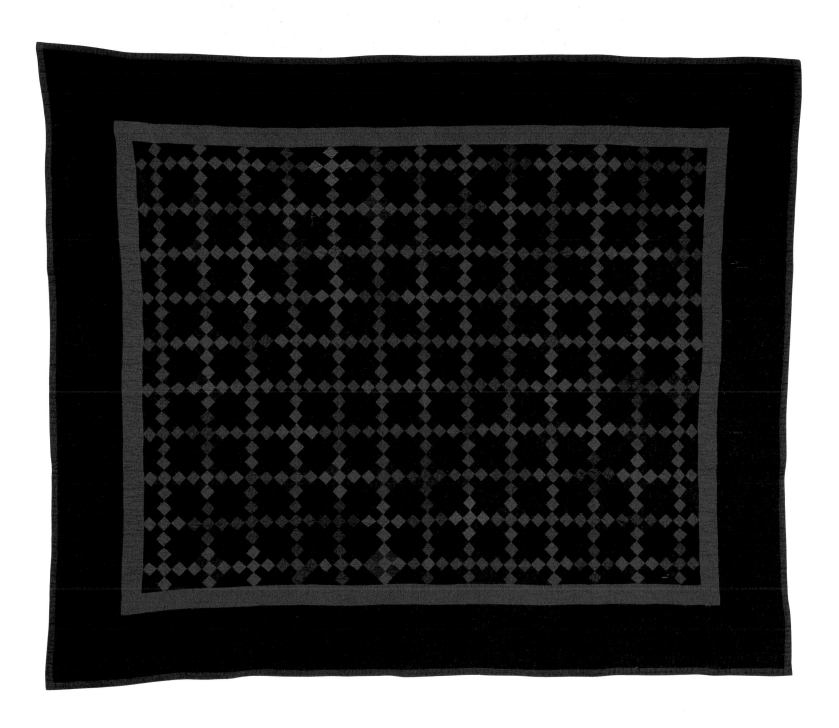

TRIPLE IRISH CHAIN

Maker unknown, 1915-1925
Holmes County, Ohio

Cotton and cotton sateen, 235.0 x 196.0 cm
Quilting patterns: cables, crosshatching, chevrons

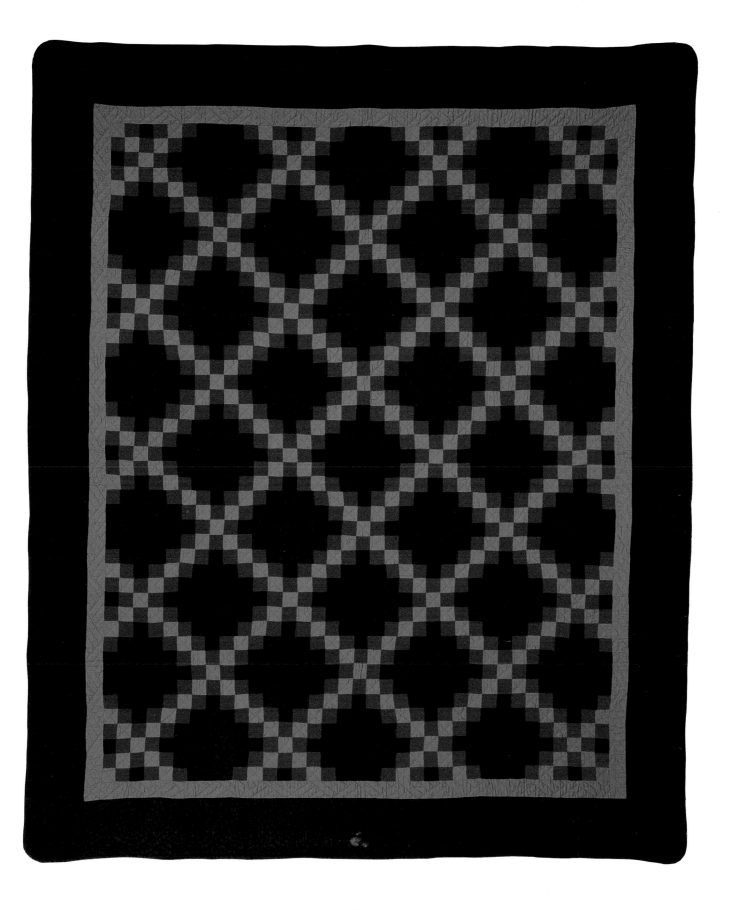

CAT. 48 (ABOVE)

BRICKS OR STREAK OF LIGHTNING

Maker unknown, 1920-1930
Ohio

Cotton, 203.2 x 175.3 cm
Quilting patterns: oval leaves and cables

CAT. 49 (OPPOSITE)

PLAIN QUILT

Maker unknown, 1920-1930
Ohio

Cotton and cotton sateen, 198.8 x 197.5 cm
Quilting patterns: rose wreaths, crosshatching, diagonal lines, tulips, cables

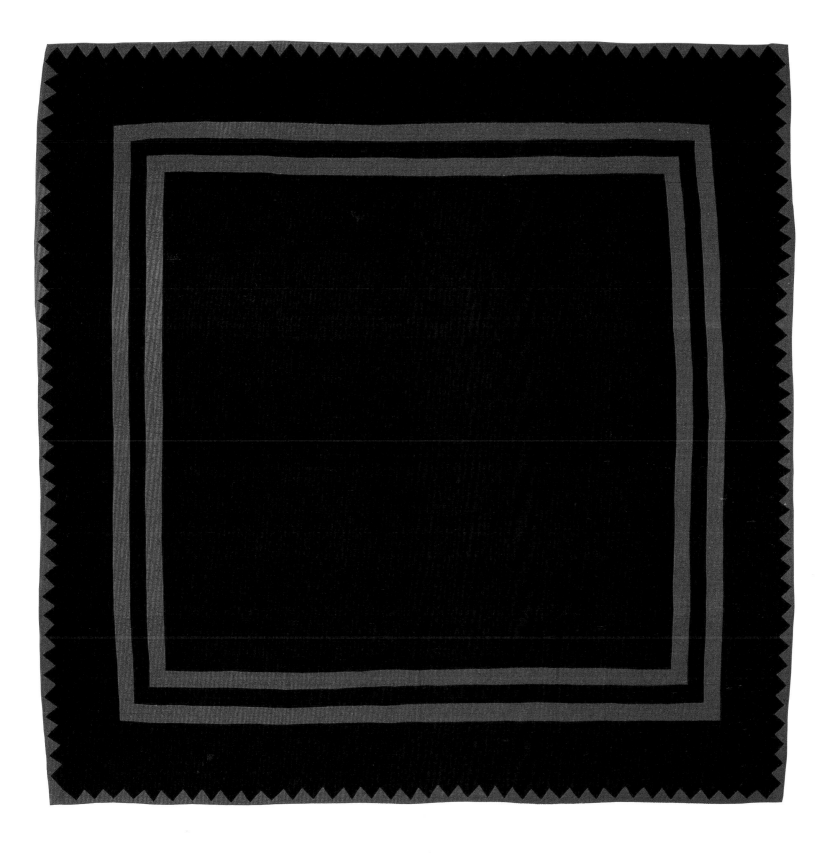

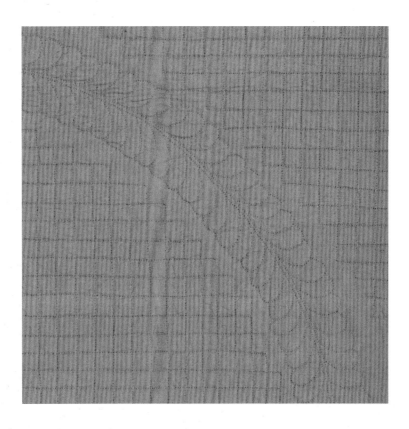

CAT. 50

FRAMED CENTER QUILT (TWO-SIDED)

Maker unknown, 1920-1930
Ohio

Cotton and cotton sateen, 196.9 x 197.5 cm
Quilting patterns: feather wreaths, crosshatching, cables, diagonal parallel lines

CAT. 51 (ABOVE)

BOW TIE

Maker unknown, 1930-1940
Holmes County, Ohio

Cotton and cotton sateen, 229.2 x 179.7 cm
Quilting patterns: interlocking ovals and diamonds, cables

CAT. 52 (OPPOSITE)

BOW TIE

Maker unknown, 1915-1925
Ohio

Wool and cotton, 188 x 190.5 cm
Quilting pattern: crosshatching

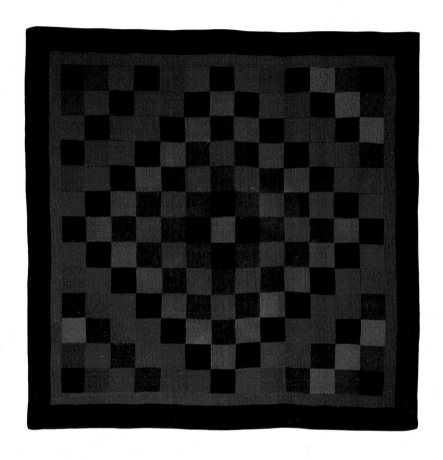

CAT. 53 (ABOVE)

SUNSHINE AND SHADOW OR ONE PATCH

Maker unknown, 1920-1930
Ohio

Wool, cotton, and cotton sateen, 196.2 x 194.3 cm
Quilting patterns: leaves, parallel lines,
feather wreaths, crosshatching

CAT. 54 (OPPOSITE)

ONE PATCH

Maker unknown, 1930-1940
Ohio

Cotton and rayon, 197 x 184 cm
Quilting pattern: concentric circles

The artist embellished the outline of the One Patch pattern
with a "turkey foot" embroidery design.

CAT. 55

STRIP STAR

Maker unknown, 1920-1940
Ohio

Cotton, 182.9 x 188 cm
Quilting patterns: parallel lines, interlocking diamonds and ovals, ropes

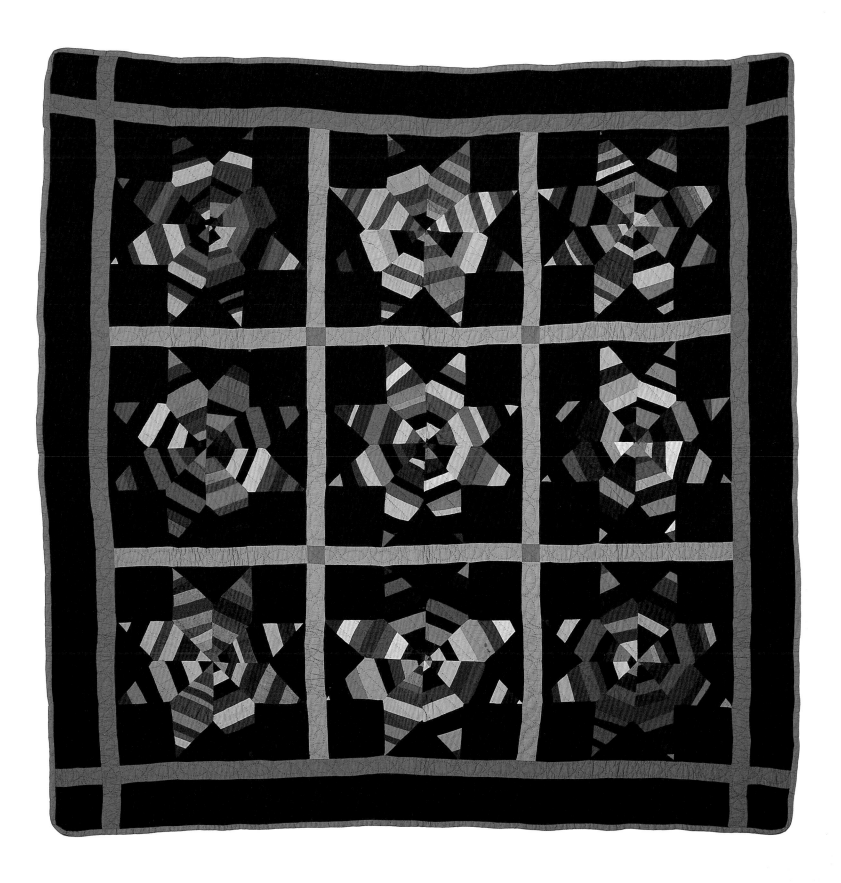

CAT. 56

BROKEN STAR

Maker unknown, 1920-1930
Ohio

Cotton, 217.8 x 214 cm
Quilting patterns: feathers, floral, fiddlehead ferns

Pub. Pellman, Rachel and Kenneth, *The World of Amish Quilts*,
Intercourse, Pennslyvania, Good Books, 1984, 52, Fig. 99.

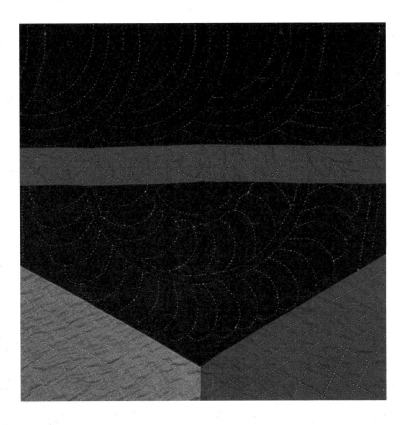

CAT. 57

STAR OF THE EAST OR **PINWHEEL**

Maker unknown, 1920-1930
Holmes County, Ohio

Cotton sateen, 166.4 x 190.5 cm
Quilting patterns: diagonal crosshatching, parallel lines,
feather wreaths, oval leaves, fans

Pub. Fisher, Laura, *Quilts of Illusion*, Pittstown, New Jersey,
The Main Street Press, 1988, p. 36-37.

CAT. 58

STAR OF BETHLEHEM

Maker unknown, 1920-1930
Holmes County, Ohio

Cotton and cotton sateen, 185.4 x 187.3 cm
Quilting patterns: crosshatching and ropes

CAT. 59
Crib Quilt
NINE PATCH

Maker unknown, 1930-1940
Ohio

Cotton, 114.3 x 89.5 cm
Quilting patterns: leaves, cables,
parallel lines, tulips

CAT. 60
Crib Quilt
BOW TIE

Maker unknown, 1925-1935
Ohio

Cotton, 92.7 x 71.8 cm
Quilting patterns: straight stitching, crosshatching,
lazy diamonds, connecting circles

CAT. 61

Crib Quilt
BASKETS

Maker unknown, 1930-1940
Ohio

Cotton, 113 x 90.8 cm
Quilting pattern: chevrons and parallel lines

CAT. 62

Crib Quilt
BARS

Maker unknown, 1920-1930
Ohio

Cotton, 125.7 x 111.8 cm
Quilting patterns: crosshatching and diamonds

CAT. 63

Crib Quilt
BRICKS (SIDE ONE, LEFT)
GEOMETRIC STRIPES (SIDE TWO, RIGHT)

Maker unknown, 1920-1930
Ohio

Cotton and wool, 95.5 x 74.5 cm
Quilting patterns: cables and crosshatching

 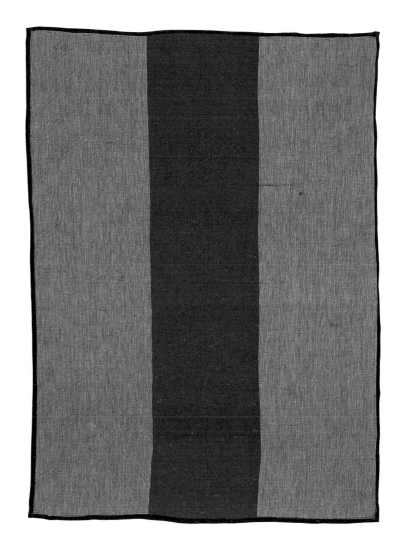

CAT. 64

Crib Quilt

WINDOW PANE OR PLAIN QUILT WITH SINGLE INNER BORDER (SIDE ONE, LEFT)
BARS (SIDE TWO, RIGHT)

Maker unknown, 1890-1900
Holmes County, Ohio

Cotton, 98.4 x 72.4 cm
Quilting patterns: feather wreaths and crosshatching

Pub. Pellman, Rachel and Kenneth, *Amish Crib Quilts*,
Intercourse, Pennsylvania, Good Books, 1985, 90.

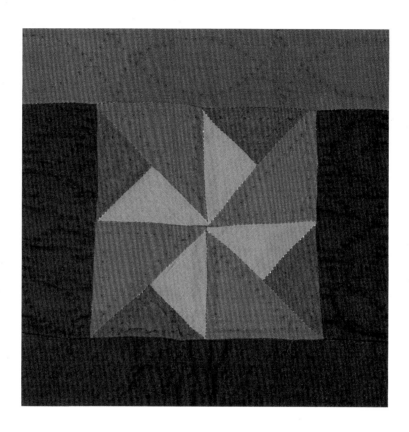

Detail of CAT. 66

CAT. 65

Doll Quilt
EIGHT POINT STARS

Maker unknown, 1920-1930
Ohio

Wool and cotton, 52.5 x 47.1 cm
Quilting pattern: ovals

CAT. 66

Crib Quilt
PINWHEELS CONTAINED

Maker unknown, 1920-1930
Ohio

Wool, cotton and cotton sateen, 88.3 x 72.4 cm
Quilting patterns: leaves and diamonds, pumpkin seeds, cables

Quilts
from Other Regions

CAT. 67 (ABOVE)

PUSS IN THE CORNER

Maker unknown, 1888
Iowa

Wool and cotton, 189.9 x 158.1 cm
Quilting patterns: cables, parallel lines, hearts, floral wreaths

The artist embroidered the initials "E.S." and quilted the date
"Aug. 1888" within the inner border.

CAT. 68 (OPPOSITE)

SAWTOOTH AND TRIANGLES

Maker unknown, 1900-1910
Iowa

Wool, 180.3 x 174.0 cm
Quilting pattern: large fans

CAT. 69

ROMAN STRIPES

Made by Kate (Sunning) Fugate, 1885-1895
Macomb, Illinois

Wool and cotton, 172.7 x 200.7 cm
There is no quilting on the front of the quilt.
The back, however, is quilted in a diagonal crosshatch design.

According to the collector's notes, the artist made the quilt
"for my father-in-law, Charlie Kost, (because) when he was a boy
he hauled my coal and helped me with my chores."

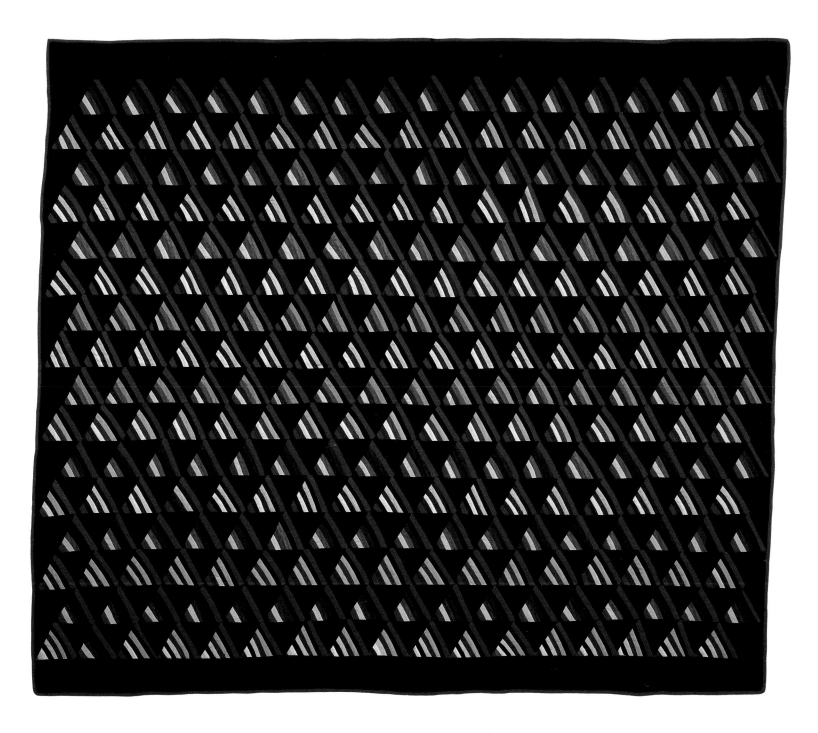

CAT. 70

FANS

Made by Lydia S. Whetstone, ca. 1934
Shipshewana, Indiana

Cotton sateen and wool, 188 x 212.7 cm
Quilting patterns: feathers and trailing tulips

The outlines of the fans are embellished with embroidery
and the date "1934" is quilted into the fabric. According to the collector's notes,
the artist made this quilt shortly before her marriage to Ammon E. Bontrager.

Pub. Pottinger, David, *Quilts from the Indiana Amish: A Regional Collection,*
New York, E.P. Dutton, Inc. in association with the Museum of American Folk Art, 1983, 39, Fig. 37.

CAT. 71

ROMAN STRIPES

Maker unknown, 1920-1935
Indiana

Wool, cotton, velvet and cotton sateen, 172.7 x 200.7 cm
Quilting patterns: half-feather wreaths, crosshatching, ropes, cables

Pub. Bishop, Robert Charles, *New Discoveries in American Quilts*,
New York, E.P. Dutton, Inc., 1975, 63, Fig. 92.

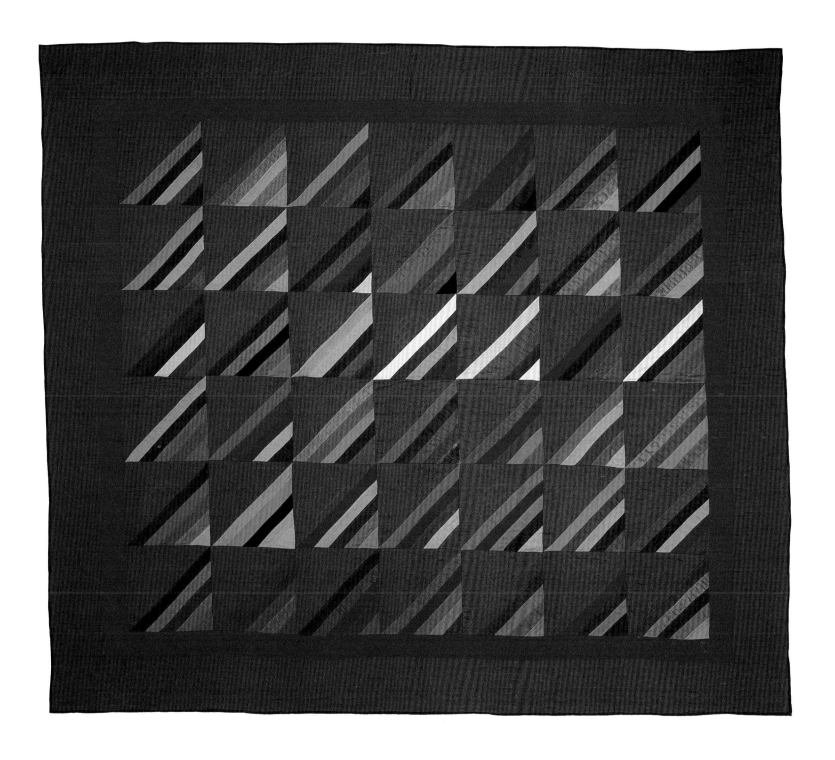

CAT. 72

Crib Quilt

HOLE IN THE BARN DOOR

Made by Fannie Miller, 1922
Nappanee, Indiana

Cotton, 147.3 x 99.7 cm
Quilting patterns: diagonal parallel lines and crosshatching

The artist made this quilt in honor of the birth of her first son, Harvey, born October 1, 1922.
According to the collector's notes, the quilt was never used and spent its entire life
in a trunk in the attic. After the death of Fanny Miller in 1989, her belongings
were divided among her two children, Harvey and Rosa, and the rest sold at auction.
Since it was made for him, Harvey received this crib quilt.

CAT. 73

BASKETS

Made by Anna Miller, 1915
Middlebury, Indiana

Cotton and cotton sateen, 221. x 175.3 cm
Quilting patterns: tulips, parallel lines, fans

Signed "Anna Miller, February 24th, 1915" in quilting on the inner border.

Pub. Pottinger, David, *Quilts from the Indiana Amish: A Regional Collection*, New York, E.P. Dutton, Inc.
in association with the Museum of American Folk Art, 1983, 44, Fig. 45.

References Cited

Bender, Sue

1989   *Plain and Simple: A Woman's Journey to the Amish*. San Francisco: Harper and Row.

Bishop, Robert, and Elizabeth Safanda

1976   *A Gallery of Amish Quilts: Design Diversity from a Plain People*. New York: E.P. Dutton & Co., Inc.

Committee of Fisher Descendants

1988   *Descendants and History of Christian Fisher (1757-1838)*. 3d ed., 361, entry 10367. Lancaster, Pa.: Eby's Quality Printing.

Deeben, John Paul

1990   "A Cultural Trait in Transition: The Agricultural Development of the Pennsylvania Amish, 1750–1920." Master's thesis, Pennsylvania State University.

Dyck, Cornelius J.

1993   *An Introduction to Mennonite History: A Popular History of the Anabaptists and the Mennonites*. 3rd ed. Scottdale, Pa.: Herald Press.

Gail, Peter

1994   "The Plain Way of Doin' Business." *Plain Communities Business Exchange* 1(6):1.

Gibbons, Phebe Earle

1872   *Pennsylvania Dutch and Other Essays*. Philadelphia: J.B. Lippencott.

Gingrich, Hugh F., and Rachel W. Kreider

1986   *Amish and Amish Mennonite Genealogies*, p. 229, entry no. KZB6341. Gordonville, Pa.: Pequea Publishers.

Godey's Lady's Book

1855   Vol. 51 (August):1-5.

1860   Vol. 61 (September):271.

Granick, Eve Wheatcroft

1989   *The Amish Quilt*. Intercourse, Pa.: Good Books.

1990   "Amish Quilts of Lancaster County." In *Amish Quilts of Lancaster County*. San Francisco: M.H. de Young Memorial Museum.

Haders, Phyllis

1976   *Sunshine and Shadow*. New York: Universe Books.

Holstein, Jonathan

1973   *The Pieced Quilt: An American Design Tradition*. Greenwich, Conn.: New York Graphic Society Ltd.

1991   "The Aesthetics of Commemorative Quilts." In *Made to Remember: American Commemorative Quilts*. Ithaca: New York: Herbert F. Johnson Museum of Art, Cornell University.

Hostetler, Beulah Stauffer

1992   "The Formation of the Old Orders." *The Mennonite Quarterly Review* 66(1):5-25.

Hostetler, John A.

1989   *Amish Roots: A Treasury of History, Wisdom and Lore*. Baltimore: The Johns Hopkins University Press.

1993   *Amish Society*. 4th ed. Baltimore: The Johns Hopkins University Press.

Hostetler, John A., and Gertrude Enders Huntington

1992   *Amish Children: Education in the Family, School, and Community*. 2d ed. Fort Worth, Tex.: Harcourt Brace Jovanovich.

Hughes, Robert, and Julie Silber

1990   *Amish: The Art of the Quilt*. New York: Alfred A. Knopf.

Huntington, Gertrude Enders

1994   "Persistence and Change in Amish Education." In *The Amish Struggle with Modernity*. Ed. Donald B. Kraybill and Marc A. Olshan. Hanover, N.H.: University Press of New England.

Hymowitz, Carol, and Michaele Weissman

1981   *A History of Women in America*. 3rd printing. New York: Bantam Books.

Keim, Albert N., ed.

1975   *Compulsory Education and the Amish: The Right Not to be Modern*. Boston: Beacon Press.

Keyser, Alan G.

1978   "Beds, Bedding, Bedsteads and Sleep," *Der Reggeboge: The Rainbow Quarterly of the Pennsylvania German Society* 12 (4):1-18. Reprinted as "Early Pennsylvania-German Bedding" in *Pieced by Mother, Symposium Papers*. Ed. Jeanette Lasansky. Lewisburg, Pa.: Oral Traditions Project, 1988.

Klimuska, Edward S.

1987   "Quilts: Lancaster County's Fastest Growing Home Industry Is Making New Quilts." Lancaster Pa.: *Lancaster New Era* series, 9-13 March, 1987. Reprinted as *Lancaster County Quilt Capital U.S.A.* Lancaster, Pa.: *Lancaster New Era*, 1987.

Kollmorgen, Walter M.

1942   "Culture of a Contemporary Community: The Old Order Amish of Lancaster County, Pennsylvania." *Rural Life Studies* 4. Washington, D.C.: Bureau of Agricultural Economics.

Kouwenhoven, John

1948   *Made in America: The Arts in Modern Civilization*. Newton, Mass.: Branford.

Kraybill, Donald B.

1989   *The Riddle of Amish Culture*. Baltimore: The Johns Hopkins University Press.

1993   *The Amish and the State*, ed. Baltimore: The Johns Hopkins University Press.

1994   "Plotting Social Change Across Four Affiliations." In *The Amish Struggle with Modernity*. Ed. Donald B. Kraybill and Marc A. Olshan. Hanover, N.H.: University Press of New England.

Kraybill, Donald B., and Lucian Niemeyer

1993   *Old Order Amish*. Baltimore: The Johns Hopkins University Press.

Kraybill, Donald B., and Steven M. Nolt

1994   "The Rise of Microenterprises." In T*he Amish Struggle with Modernity*. Ed. Donald B. Kraybill and Marc A. Olshan. Hanover, N.H.: University Press of New England.

1995   *Amish Enterprise: From Plows to Profits*. Baltimore: The Johns Hopkins University Press.

Kraybill, Donald B., and Marc A. Olshan, ed.

1994   *The Amish Struggle with Modernity*. Hanover, N.H.: University Press of New England.

Larkin, Jack

1988   *The Reshaping of Everyday Life*. New York: Harper and Row.

Lerner, Gerda

1979   "The Lady and the Mill Girl." In *A Heritage of Her Own: Toward a New Social History of American Women*. New York: Simon and Schuster.

Lichten, Frances

1946   *Folk Art of Rural Pennsylvania*. New York: Charles Scribner's Sons.

Luthy, David

1994   "Amish Migration Patterns: 1972-1992." In *The Amish Struggle with Modernity*. Ed. Donald B. Kraybill and Marc A. Olshan. Hanover, N.H.: University Press of New England.

Macleish, Archibald

1972   "If Life Means Going Without, The Amish Go Without." Excerpted from "Rediscovering the Simple Life." *McCall's* (April), 79-88.

Mast, Lois Ann

1991   *The Peter Leibundgutt Journal*, p. 29, no. 8. Elverson, Pa.: Mennonite Family History.

McCauley, Daniel and Kathryn

1988   *Decorative Arts of the Amish of Lancaster County*. Intercourse, Pa.: Good Books.

Mennonite Encyclopedia, The

1956   Five vols. Scottdale, Pa.: Mennonite Publishing House; Hillsboro, Kans.: Mennonite Brethren Publishing House; Newton, Kans.: Mennonite Publication Office.

Meyers, Thomas J.

1993   "Education and Schooling." In *The Amish and the State*. Ed. Donald B. Kraybill. Baltimore: The Johns Hopkins University Press.

1994   "Lunch Pails and Factories." In *The Amish Struggle with Modernity*. Ed. Donald B. Kraybill and Marc A. Olshan. Hanover, N.H.: University Press of New England.

Nolt, Steven M.

1992   *A History of the Amish*. Intercourse, Pa.: Good Books.

Olshan, Marc A.

1980   "Strangely Primitive." Excerpted from "The Old Order Amish as a Model for Development." Doctoral dissertation, Cornell University.

1993   "The National Amish Steering Committee." In *The Amish and the State*. Ed. Donald B. Kraybill. Baltimore: The Johns Hopkins University Press.

1994a   "Homespun Bureaucracies: A Case Study in Organizational Evolution." In *The Amish Struggle with Modernity*. Ed. Donald B. Kraybill and Marc A. Olshan. Hanover, N.H.: University Press of New England.

1994b   "Amish Cottage Industries as Trojan Horse." In *The Amish Struggle with Modernity*. Ed. Donald B. Kraybill and Marc A. Olshan. Hanover, N.H.: University Press of New England.

Olshan, Marc A., and Kimberly Schmidt

1994   "Amish Women and the Feminist Conundrum." In *The Amish Struggle with Modernity*. Ed. Donald B. Kraybill and Marc A. Olshan. Hanover, N.H.: University Press of New England.

Orlofsky, Patsy and Myron

1974   *Quilts in America*. New York: McGraw-Hill.

Osler, Dorothy

1987   *Traditional British Quilts*. London: B.T. Batsford Ltd.

Pellman, Rachel and Kenneth

1984   *The World of Amish Quilts*. Intercourse, Pa.: Good Books.

1985   *Amish Crib Quilts*. Intercourse, Pa.: Good Books.

Pottinger, David

1983   *Quilts from the Indiana Amish: A Regional Collection*. New York: E.P. Dutton in association with the Museum of Modern Folk Art, New York.

Photograph and Illustration Credits

Roth, John D., ed. and trans.

1993   *Letters of the Amish Division: A Source Book.* Goshen, Ind.: Mennonite Historical Society.

Safanda, Elizabeth, and Robert Bishop

1976   *A Gallery of Amish Quilts: Design Diversity from a Plain People.* New York: E.P. Dutton & Co., Inc.

Scott, Stephen

1986   *Why Do They Dress That Way?* Intercourse, Pa.: Good Books.

1988   *The Amish Wedding and Other Special Occasions of the Old Order Communities.* Intercourse, Pa.: Good Books.

Yoder, Paton

1991   *Tradition & Transition: Amish Mennonites and Old Order Amish 1800-1900.* Scottdale, Pa.: Herald Press.

1993   "The Amish View of the State." In *The Amish and the State.* Ed. Donald B. Kraybill. Baltimore: The Johns Hopkins University Press.

All studio photographs are by Denis J. Nervig, unless otherwise noted.

PAGE 11. Map designed by Anthony A. G. Kluck.
1. Reprinted by permission of Good Books, Intercourse, Pa.
16. Drawing by Patrick Fitzgerald, after an illustration provided courtesy of the Pennsylvania German Society.
17, 18, 19. Photograph by Jonathan Charles.
20. Courtesy of Indiana State Museum.
21. Photograph by Jonathan Charles. Reprinted by permission of Good Books, Intercourse, Pa.
22. Rephotographed by Jonathan Charles.
23. Photograph by Jonathan Charles.
24. Photograph by Jonathan Charles. Courtesy of Kathryn and Daniel McCauley.
29, 30. Photographs by Jonathan Charles.
31. Rephotographed by Jonathan Charles.
32, 33, 34, 35. Reprinted by permission of Good Books, Intercourse, Pa.
36. Rephotographed by Jonathan Charles.
37. Photograph by Jonathan Charles.
38. Rephotographed by Jonathan Charles.
39. Courtesy of Jonathan Holstein.
40. Courtesy of America Hurrah Archive, NYC.
41. Courtesy of New York State Historical Association, Cooperstown, N.Y.
42. Courtesy of the Mount Vernon Ladies' Association, Mount Vernon, Va.
43. Courtesy of Jonathan Holstein.
45, 61. Courtesy of America Hurrah Archive, NYC.
62. Courtesy of Jonathan Holstein.

FRONT COVER, TOP TO BOTTOM: CAT. 2, CAT. 58, CAT 68.

PAGE 3: Detail of CAT. 2.

PAGE 5 (DEDICATION): An elder Amish man pays homage to personal rites of passage by displaying private momentos upon his dresser. Included are a marriage certificate and water tumbler set used to serve his wedding party as well as memorials in honor of his parents and other family members. Photograph by Susan Einstein, Elkhart-LaGrange Counties, Indiana, 1981-1984.

PAGE 6: Barn interior. Photograph by Susan Einstein, Elkhart-LaGrange Counties, Indiana, 1981-1984.

PAGE 8: Amish girls climb into their buggy for the ride home after Church services. Photograph by Susan Einstein, Elkhart-LaGrange Counties, Indiana, 1981-1984.

PAGE 232: Photograph by Susan Einstein, Elkhart-LaGrange Counties, Indiana, 1981-1984.

BACK COVER: Detail of CAT. 56.

Contributors to this Volume

DONALD B. KRAYBILL, PH.D., is Professor of Sociology and Anabaptist-Pietist studies at Messiah College, Pennsylvania, where he also serves as provost. His numerous publications on Amish culture include *The Riddle of Amish Culture* (The Johns Hopkins University Press, 1989), *The Amish and the State* (The Johns Hopkins University Press, 1993), *The Amish Struggle with Modernity* (University Press of New England, 1994), and *Amish Enterprise: From Plows to Profits* (The Johns Hopkins University Press, 1995).

PATRICIA T. HERR, a researcher, lecturer, and collector of Pennsylvania historic textiles, has curated exhibits sponsored by the Heritage Center Museum of Lancaster, Philadelphia Museum of Art, and Winterthur Museum. She serves on the Advisory Committee of the Philadelphia Museum of Art's Costume and Textile Department and has been actively involved as a board member and volunteer for the Landis Valley Museum and the Heritage Center Museum. Her articles on textiles have appeared in *Early American Life, The Quilt Digest, The Magazine Antiques,* quilt symposium proceedings, and museum publications. She recently authored the book, *"The Ornamental Branches": Needlework and Arts from the Lititz Moravian Girls' School Between 1800 and 1865.* Dr. Herr is a practicing companion animal veterinarian.

JONATHAN HOLSTEIN's interest in quilts has been as a collector, curator of exhibitions, lecturer, and writer; he is particularly interested in their aesthetics. In 1971 he and his wife curated "Abstract Design in American Quilts" at the Whitney Museum of Art in New York which, with his subsequent work, is seen as pivotal in the creation of the modern worldwide interest in quilts and quilting. Scores of other exhibitions followed, the most recent being "Uncommon Quilts" at the Fenimore House Museum, New York State Historical Association, Cooperstown, New York (April through December 1996). His many publications include *American Pieced Quilts* (Editions des Massons, 1972), *The Pieced Quilt: An American Design Tradition* (New York Graphic Society, 1973) and *Abstract Design in American Quilts: A Biography of an Exhibition* (The Kentucky Quilt Project, 1991). He was a founder and editor of *The Quilt Journal: An International Review,* and is currently on the Advisory Council of The Alliance for American Quilts, which is working toward the establishment of a national quilt center.

SUSAN EINSTEIN, M.A., is a commercial photographer who lived in an Amish community for several years. She specializes in photography of art objects for museums and galleries. She received a Masters in Art History from University of California, Berkeley.